THE MILLIGAN PAPERS

John Antrobus

The Milligan Papers
© 2019. John Antrobus. All rights reserved.

All illustrations are copyright of their respective owners, and are also reproduced here in the spirit of publicity. Whilst we have made every effort to acknowledge specific credits whenever possible, we apologize for any omissions, and will undertake every effort to make any appropriate changes in future editions of this book if necessary.

No part of this book may be reproduced in any form or by any means, electronic, mechanical, digital, photocopying or recording, except for the inclusion in a review, without permission in writing from the publisher.

Published in the USA by:
BearManor Media
P O Box 71426
Albany, Georgia 31708
www.bearmanormedia.com

Printed in the United States of America

ISBN   978-1-62933-434-9 (paperback)
        978-1-62933-435-6 (hardcover)

Book and cover design by Darlene Swanson • www.van-garde.com

THE MILLIGAN PAPERS

THE MILLIGAN PAPERS was FIRST BROADCAST for BBC Radio 4 on 28th January 1987, and was a series of six weekly comedy half hour episodes.

What, really? That's quite a long time ago, like over thirty years, so what's new?

OK, what's new is that the scripts have been adapted by John Hewer and myself for a stage show and that opened with a tour of one night stands in the North of England late 2018. As the company all returned safely with their van relatively unmarked we assume it was a great success.

Back to 1987!

The cast of stars, plucked from the Heavens and Balham Labour Exchange were led over the cliffs into imbecility by,

SPIKE MILLIGAN

Followed by,
JOHN BLUTHAL
CHRIS LANGHAM
JOHN ANTROBUS.

Announcements by EUGENE FRASER.

The MUSIC was by Kenny Ball and his Jazzmen (Episode One) and George Chisholm and his Gentlemen Of Jazz (Episodes One to Six)

The writer was JOHN ANTROBUS.

The producer was PAUL SPENSER.

The audience was Fred who claims he is still suffering from dizzy spells but as he could never spell dizzy before that is an improvement...

A big thanks to Ben Ohmart who is mad enough to publish this book with my illustrations. And to Darlene Swanson who with Divine Patience designed the book beautifully. Ben is based in Japan and Darlene in Florida so no matter the time there's always someone to talk to!

NOTE: Any enquiries regarding the stage adaptation please make to Jean Diamond Management.

> *'Faith is the substance of things hoped for,*
> *The evidence of things not yet seen...'*
> St Paul

A book is an ex-tree on the way to a landfill without the intervention of the reader. The reader makes the book. She / He has been given the gift of literacy and over the centuries many courageous souls fought for that universal franchise against the deep mysteries of religion holding literacy as a secret priestly art...

"I condemn you to be burnt at the stake for practising the unlicensed art of reading. It is much too dangerous for the unsanctified mind to practise. If let be soon the whole world will be reading! Imagine that if you can! On various instruments of communication which have yet to be invented! Be sure it will be the devils work satisfying this habit with authors springing up everywhere to provide entertainment! Heaven forbid! Take them away..."

Like everything else nothing goes beyond the cloudburst of an idea except through faith. You can move your own mountains through faith. Your own dreams are the whispering of Creation. Take heart and follow your own song! The world is waiting...

> *'All things be ready if the mind be so...'*
> Will Shakespeare.

On with show, folks!

The poet William Megonagall plays to a goat—

"Och, the mee! The ni! The noo!"
"I am a bonny poet—
Though the world has yet
to know it—
Oh aye the nooo—!!"

THE MILLIGAN PAPERS

With an introduction by the Scottish poet, William Mcgonagal

Ohhhhhh study the table of contents well,
For the titles do the lives foretell...
Proving that Destiny has no bending,
So best to hope for Happy Endings...
There are many fine characters included here
Including William Mcgonagall who does not drink beer!
Descended from the mountain peaks
Where he was reciting to goats for several weeks.
Though the goats were not much moved
My diction was certainly improved!
I walked to London from a far green glen
Worn down to my knees by the time I saw Big Ben!
But when I was hired by the BBC
My situation improved to one of dire poverty...
Ohhhhh! Och, aye, nose and teeth!!

The Milligan Papers

Episode One: THE CASE OF THE DISAPPEARING FLYING SCOTSMAN 1

Episode Two: JONAH AND THE WHALE 29

Episode Three: FROM RAGS TO MORE RAGS 59

Episode Four: THAT CAKE-ELUSIVE PIMPERNEL 89

Episode Five: THE INCURABLES—PART ONE 117

Episode Six: THE INCURABLES—PART TWO 143

Spike in a good mood— promising!

INTRODUCTION

WELCOME to the grand MILLIGAN adventure, the highs the lows of six mad, mad Sundays recorded before a live audience (according to their medical reports) at the Paris Theatre, Lower Regent Street, in the heart liver and kidneys of London—actually just off Piccadilly Circus where tourists gathered under the darting arrows of the statue of Eros and fell in love or lust.

The year was 1987 and Britain was busy packaging and exporting it to nations that had little sense of time—not realizing how lucky they were…

A foreman explained, "We've just sent a fortnight to Senegal, actually it's a remnant from 1953 but they won't notice!"

Thus, the brutality of capitalism. But let the absurdity lie hopefully in the pages unfolding in the six scripts of this BBC radio series. The whole concept I sold to the Beeb around the name of Spike Milligan. So there I was, also busy packaging a friend into six comedy half hours for the air waves. Well, I had his permission to do so. The famous Goon Show was done, though still repeated through the years, and I did not set myself up to compete with that jewel in the crown of the BBC.

The Milligan Papers

I thought to write my own absurd stories, six of them, and use the immense talents of Spike to feature in them, and bless us with success. I knew not what monster or saint I was letting loose upon those quiet Sunday afternoons. Innocent or blind I took the commission with gratitude.

Perhaps my scribbled notes upon the pages of the scripts, before and after each show give some idea of the Heaven and hell of it, the hope and despair of those hours. These are imagined jottings, true, but carried me back to those days unlocking the trauma of it all I still carried in every cell of my being! Along with the history of mankind, but let's not get into that...

And so, dear reader, unless you imagine yourselves as listener, gather round the fire of pained energy burning, clearing, at last again transformed into laughter—that salve to all ills!

I confess that, for your further entertainment, I have added a few words to the scripts, bearing in mind also that the formidable actor/director/ producer John Hewer is e'en now adapting the scripts into a stage show!

Thanks to the admirable contributions to those Sundays from the talented comedy thespians John Bluthal and Chris Langham—with the remnants of gratitude for my own contribution.

And thanks to Kenny Ball and his jazzmen (Episode One only) and to George Chisholm and his Gentlemen of jazz (Episodes Two to Six) who even now are warming us up for the show of shows...

Eugene Fraser shouts, "Over here! I did the announcements, remember?" Yes, and thanks for your strange employment with us. Hopefully it has not ruined your BBC pension plan.

Hold!

Who is that ghost that lurks in the shadows? It is indeed the mega-talented producer, Paul Spencer, who somehow survived those scathing Sundays though at what cost only he could tell you. Through chattering teeth and shaking bones the spectre cries out, "Ahhh, the FUN of it all...!"

AND LASTLY A HUGE THANKS TO SPIKE MILLIGAN, FOR WITHOUT HIS TOWERING GENIUS THERE WOULD ONLY HAVE BEEN THE SOUND OF SILENCE!!!

So tune in! Be there or be square! On with the show....

In LOVE and LAUGHTER....

John.. (27th August, 2018 / This day imported from the EU, no added VAT)

This book contains no genetically modified jokes. I would also like to claim that any spelling errors are as the radio scripts came to us on the day of rehearsal when our attention was not upon its literary merit but whether in hacking it about and scrawling indecipherable additions we would get the laughs required of a comedy show. An introduction can never end, it can only lead on to the show so let the hook appear and pull me off-stage!

EPISODE 1
THE CASE OF THE DISAPPEARING FLYING SCOTSMAN

How will Spike turn up today? As the magnificent yet benevolent genius, even stooping to be humble, a mate amongst mates? Or as Gulliver tied down hair by hair by us uncomprehending Lilliputians?

Spike enters rehearsal for read-through with a smile! This is promising. He is the consummate actor but which version of Spike Milligan will he be playing today?

ANNOUNCER
The BBC Presents The Milligan Papers written by John Antrobus.

GRAMS IN STRONG

ANNOUNCER
Episode 1—The Case of the Disappearing Flying Scotsman.

(SFX: Train pulling away from station.)

MILLIGAN
Stop! Stop that train! Stop! Stop! Stop thief!

(SFX: POLICE CAR.)

MILLIGAN
Listen— a sound effect!

INSPECTOR
Are you the gentleman who called for Scotland Yard?

MILLIGAN
Yes.

INSPECTOR
Can I take your name?

MILLIGAN
No. If I did that, what would I use?

INSPECTOR
When did you last see the train?

MILLIGAN
On platform 7.

INSPECTOR
Have you a description of it?

MILLIGAN
Yes...

INSPECTOR
...Describe it then.

MILLIGAN
It's made of concrete.

INSPECTOR
The train is made of concrete?

MILLIGAN

Is it? You could've fooled me. Mind you, anyone could fool me. It's the same as the platform, then.

INSPECTOR

Did you see who took the train, Mr. Blabb?

MILLIGAN

Yes, I got a good look at them. There was about a hundred of them, all sitting down in the carriages. I didn't like the look of them. Next thing you know, the train is steaming out of the station. WOOOOO! Chu-chu-chu-chu-chu-chu...

INSPECTOR

We're much obliged to you, Mr. Blabb.

MILLIGAN

Thank you, Inspector. You see, there's a lot of trains pilfered from Kings Cross, sir. You turn your back and... WOOOOO! Chu-chu-chu-chu-chu-chu... They're gone!

INSPECTOR

Do you think it's the same gang every time?

MILLIGAN

It could be, sir. It's scandalous. The authorities are always replacing the trains.

INSPECTOR

What is your present address, Mr. Blabb?

MILLIGAN

Platform 3. It's one of the better platforms, you know. But, it's the uncertainty I hate, you see. The train standing there, it's a joy to behold. Then they come again. They start sneaking up with their luggage.

INSPECTOR
Which direction do you think they were heading?

MILLIGAN
Crewe.

INSPECTOR
We'll have Crewe watched.

MILLIGAN
Could you have my knees watched as well? They have been going for walks to strange places and I have followed them.

INSPECTOR
I trust you're not telling us how to do our work, Mr. Blabb?

MILLIGAN
I didn't know you did any work. I thought you were a policeman.

INSPECTOR
Tell me, are you employed?

MILLIGAN
Not to my knowledge.

INSPECTOR
What was your previous occupation?

MILLIGAN
France. 1944. D—Day.

INSPECTOR
Were you decorated during the war?

MILLIGAN
Yes, but it's starting to peel off.

INSPECTOR
Do you have a war record?

MILLIGAN
Yes, sir.

GRAMS
"WE'LL MEET AGAIN"

ANNOUNCER
As the rumoured Flying Scotsman was speeding towards Crewe, the government took immediate action. In the House of Commons, an emergency debate raged.

OMNES
Order! Order! / One bedpan ordered, over here. / Just look at that? My God, it's enormous! / You've just trodden in it, etc., etc.

MILLIGAN
The Right Honourable Member for Crewe will rise.

RT. HON.
Oh no I won't!

MILLIGAN
Oh? But you wanted to speak?

RT. HON.
I can do that perfectly well lying down. And with Joan Collins.

OMNES
Withdraw, withdraw, etc.

RT. HON.
I can't withdraw!

MINISTER #1
What about the Flying Scotsman?

OMNES
Yes. / Hear, hear. / Where, where?

MINISTER #2
Where is it? Resign! Where is it?

MILLIGAN
Silence in the house for the Prime Minister!

CHURCHILL
We will not be bullied by the opposition. I can assure the house that the Flying Scotsman is exactly where it is at this moment. How can it possibly be anywhere else?

RT. HON.
Will the Honourable Member tell me, honestly, without prevarication, is it true what they say about Dixy? Does the sun really shine all the time?

OMNES (sung)
"Do the sweet magnolias blossom at everybody's door? Do folks keep eating possum…"

GRAMS

ANNOUNCER
Meanwhile, in a government training school for Crewe-Watching, two men were completing their course in utter secrecy.

(SFX: DUCK QUACKS)

OFFICIAL #1
What does it look like to you?

OFFICIAL #2
Errrr... Catford.

(SFX: DUCK QUACKS)

OFFICIAL #1
Catford, eh?

OFFICIAL #2
Catford, disguised as a duck. Watch out, something's coming!

An MI 5 operative —
trainspotting, disguised as a duck...
~~Risky~~ Risky in the mating season!

(SFX: TRAIN PULLS UP. DUCK QUACK. TRAIN PULLS AWAY. DUCK QUACKING OFF IN DISTANCE.)

OFFICIAL #1
Still of the same opinion, are you?

OFFICIAL #2
Well, I, erm..

OFFICIAL #1
Why would the Flying Scotsman stop at a duck?...

OFFICIAL #2
To let the people off the train.

OFFICIAL #1
Yes, that's good, yes. Put that in the report, yes. Why would people want to get off at a duck?

OFFICIAL #2
Well they'd have to, if they'd only booked that far.

OFFICIAL #1
You're right again, that's awfully good. And you're wearing the suit.

OFFICIAL #2
Thank you.

OFFICIAL #1
My time for it. You can get undressed behind that smokescreen.

OFFICIAL #2
Thanks! Did you notice something very unusual, about that sighting?

OFFICIAL #1
Like what?

OFFICIAL #2
Well, when some people got off the Flying Scotsman, the duck got on.

OFFICIAL #1
Blimey! You mean?

OFFICIAL #2

Yes, I do mean – Where's Catford gone?!

GRAMS.

OMNES
Order! Order! Etc.

MILLIGAN
Order! Order! Catford has disappeared! We demand an explanation!

MINISTER #2
I haven't got any.

MILLIGAN
We don't wish to know that, Minister. Silence in the house for the Prime Minister. What are your views on an explanation?

CHURCHILL
Well an explanation is when you tell people what's happened.

MILLIGAN
Oh, thank you, yes.

MINISTER #1
Is it true that the Ministry of Defense disguised Catford as a duck for a NATO exercise and then ate it?

OMNES
Shame! Shames! etc.

GRAMS

(SFX: TRAIN STATION. NASTY, EXUBERANT, GROTESQUE COUGHING.)

MILLIGAN
Oh, mate! That's a nasty cough you've got there, mate!

COUGHER
It's the best I can manage, mate. (COUGHS)

MILLIGAN
I think it's a very good cough, considering that you are well.

COUGHER
Yes, mate. Why should only ill people have something wrong with them? I mean, I've got to have something to complain about as well, mate.

MILLIGAN
Well you can complain to the National Health Service about that cough.

COUGHER
Why? There's nothing wrong with it! (COUGHS; Aside) It's a gift you know, it's a gift.

MILLIGAN
It's a perfectly good cough, don't get me wrong. Where did you get it?

COUGHER
The doctors, mate. I went in and … (COUGHS) It sort of takes you by surprise.

MILLIGAN
Can I try it?

COUGHER

If you like, mate.

(MILLIGAN tries to cough.)

MILLIGAN

It's a good one, all right.

COUGHER

Yes, if you don't mind me saying, you've got to get into it a bit more, mate.

(MILLIGAN coughs again.)

MILLIGAN

This is a good cough, this is.

COUGHER

Well how much would you give me for it?

MILLIGAN

Nothing.

COUGHER

Oh, I'll have it back then.

MILLIGAN

I can go down to the doctor's and get a free cough, mate.

COUGHER

What brings you here to the station anyway, mate?

MILLIGAN

My feet, mate, that's what. I come down here to wait.

COUGHER

Well this here is the waiting room, mate. So are you waiting for a train to come in or are you waiting for a free cough, mate?

MILLIGAN

I'm just waiting, mate. I'm a purist.

COUGHER

They won't let you use the waiting room just for waiting, you know. These station police will bung you out, mate.

MILLIGAN

Oh, I expect to be persecuted for my ideas. As a waiter. Not as a waiter but as a waiter! One day, people will come to waiting rooms and they'll just wait. You'll see. People will just come down here and wait.

COUGHER

What—wait to die?

MILLIGAN

To-die, tomorrow? No, that would be cheating.

COUGHER

If they waited long enough, mate, they would die.

MILLIGAN

Yes, but that's one of the hazards of the waiting profession. People in the waiting career often die before the job's finished.

COUGHER

But, but, what about the people who come in here waiting for trains, mate?

MILLIGAN

Oh, traditionalists? Well, we would reason with them and if it didn't work…

COUGHER

Yes?

MILLIGAN

We'd hit 'em.

COUGHER

How would you know the ones to hit, mate?

MILLIGAN

What?

COUGHER

How can you tell the difference between the ones waiting for the trains and the ones waiting to wait?

MILLIGAN

We'd hit the lot of them. That way, no one feels left out.

COUGHER

Oh. It's going to be a new world, is it?

MILLIGAN

Yes. It's going to be beautiful to behold. Like a massage parlour.

MAN

Oh that's a relief. Will they still let you sit on the radiators though, mate?

MILLIGAN

Oh no. Sitting on radiators is not compulsory.

(SFX: DOOR OPEN. STORM EFFECT. DOOR CLOSE.)

ANNOUNCER

Excuse me. Do you mind if I wait here?

MILLIGAN

No, no.

ANNOUNCER

If you'd just move along the radiator, I'd be much obliged.

MILLIGAN
Move along, Clarence.

COUGHER
Right, mate.

(SFX: SMASH, CLATTER)

COUGHER
Ow!

MILLIGAN
That's an awful spell of weather outside, sir.

ANNOUNCER
It's spelt quite correctly, actually. That's my weather. I always bring my own weather with me for dramatic effect. For entrances and exits, you know. I mean, when an ordinary person goes out of that door, it's like this…

(SFX: DOOR OPEN. SILENCE. DOOR CLOSE.)

ANNOUNCER
But when I go out, it's like this!

(SFX: DOOR OPEN. COMMOTION. DOOR CLOSE.)

MILLIGAN
He's gone!

(SFX: DOOR OPEN. COMMOTION. DOOR CLOSE.)

MILLIGAN
He's back!

ANNOUNCER
Move along the radiator, will you.

MILLIGAN
Move along, Clarence.

COUGHER
Right, mate.

(SFX: SMASH / CLATTER)

COUGHER
Ow!

MILLIGAN
What are you waiting for?

ANNOUNCER
I'm waiting to make an announcement.

MILLIGAN
Oh, a station announcement!

ANNOUNCEMENT
No, a radio announcement. I'm with the BBC.

MILLIGAN
Oh, you've got influences in high places, have you?

ANNOUNCEMENT
No, I'm with the BBC.

MILLIGAN
Oh, is there anything you can take for that?

ANNOUNCEMENT
No, it's incurable. You see, I'm working on The Milligan Papers. We're planning to do it Russian and threaten Moscow.

MILLIGAN
Well it's cheaper than Trident.

ANNOUNCEMENT
Also cheaper than Trident, but only just, is Kenny Ball and his Jazzmen!

KENNY BALL INTERLUDE

EVIL MASTERMIND
Where is the Flying Scottish-man?

COWERER
We're having trouble getting it to you, Lord of the Galaxy.

EVIL MASTERMIND
But it would complete my train set...

COWERER
We realize that, My Lord, your Worshipfulness, grovel-grovel.

EVIL MASTERMIND
Return to Earth and secure the Flying Scottish-man for me or you will soon be back on a BBC announcer's salary.

COWERER
No, no! Not that! No one can live on that! Not even a BBC announcer!

GRAMS—CORNY JOKE

ANNOUNCER
Meanwhile, back at the King's Cross Police Station...

MILLIGAN
What am I doing at the back of the King's Cross Police Station?

(SFX: DOOR OPEN. DOOR CLOSE.)

MILLIGAN
You want to see me, Inspector?

INSPECTOR
Yes I do.

MILLIGAN
Then I will remove your blindfold.

INSPECTOR
Thank you. I wear it for patriotic reasons.

MILLIGAN
Yes, it's not good to see what's going on a lot of the time.

INSPECTOR
Aye. Thank you for calling in on me at the yard.

MILLIGAN
Well it was easy, when you're clubbed, handcuffed, and dragged in.

INSPECTOR
Ah, so you found your own way?

MILLIGAN
I did.

INSPECTOR
Welcome to the questioning room.

MILLIGAN
But what am I doing here?

INSPECTOR
That is the question. Would you mind untying me from this chair?

MILLIGAN
Untying people from chairs is my hobby. It's my pleasure.

INSPECTOR
It is my pleasure as well.

MILLIGAN
Kinky, eh? *

INSPECTOR
No, I have a fear of falling to the floor. That is why I get my men to tie me up every morning.

MILLIGAN
What, nude?

INSPECTOR
Not all of them. You have to ignore the truncheons, of course.

MILLIGAN
It's as well to take every precaution.

INSPECTOR
Now, do you recognise the person in this photograph?

MILLIGAN
Yes, it's my wife.

INSPECTOR
It's my wife as well.

MILLIGAN

I wondered where she'd got to these last 28 years… There's a lot of washing up and socks in the sink.

INSPECTOR

We have a report from the King's Cross station police here. Apparently you're starting a dangerous new sect in the waiting room?

MILLIGAN

Yes, apparently I'm starting a dangerous new sect—

INSPECTOR & MILLIGAN

in the waiting room.

MILLIGAN

It's called the apparently dangerous new set in the waiting room sect.

INSPECTOR

You're waiting for the 5:25 to Coulsdon South then?

MILLIGAN

Don't tell the passengers; it would raise their beliefs in British Rail! No, we just do readings from the old timetables.

INSPECTOR

Southern region?

MILLIGAN

Well they are the old favourites, yes. And we start every service with a hymn.

(**Sings**)
"Passengers will please refrain,
From passing water on the train
While it's standing in the station yard

INSPECTOR

(Sings)

"We encourage constipation

While the train is in the station—

MILLIGAN

Don't go on! Don't go on! There's people listening. We don't sing the second verse.

INSPECTOR

It was you, Mr Blabb, who reported the Flying Scotsman had gone missing.

MILLIGAN

Yes... or to put it another way... (SPIKE adlibs noises)

INSPECTOR

Would you be prepared to disguise yourself as Crewe station?

MILLIGAN

I would much like to disguise myself as Crewe station. Do you think a ginger beard and a spotted jockstrap would do the trick?

INSPECTOR

Yes. Would you be prepared to sign the official secrets act?

MILLIGAN

Would you be prepared to show it to me?

INSPECTOR

No.

MILLIGAN

Then I must refuse.

INSPECTOR

On the grounds of conscience?

MILLIGAN

No, on the grounds of cruelty that you would not let a man with a spotted beard and a ginger jockstrap…. (SPIKE cracks up; to audience) Take it as read!

INSPECTOR

Good heavens, man! If you care that much you could see it every weekend for 3 hours. You could take it to the zoo.

MILLIGAN

Oooh. I would love to take the official secrets act to the zoo.

GRAMS

ANNOUNCER

As Mr. Blabb returned the official secrets act to Whitehall and hastily donned his disguise, he realised he was already too late, for the Flying Scotsman was already drawing out of Crewe station.

(SFX: TRAIN PULLING AWAY FROM STATION)

MILLIGAN

Stop! Stop that train! Stop thief!

(SFX: POLICE BELL APPROACHING)

INSPECTOR

We have decided to disguise you as Glasgow Central further up the line.

MILLIGAN

I couldn't stand the disgrace. I promised my mother I would never disguise myself as Glasgow Central.

INSPECTOR

But you'd be doing it for your country!

MILLIGAN

I promised my mother I would never do it for my country. We have to think of the neighbours you know.

INSPECTOR

I don't know any neighbours.

MILLIGAN

Yes you do, just none that you can think of!

GRAMS—CORNY JOKE

INSPECTOR

Mr. Blabb, we don't know what's going on.

MILLIGAN

Neither do the audience by the sound of it...

INSPECTOR

But here at the yard, we're baffled.

MILLIGAN

Well, it keeps the heat in during the winter.

INSPECTOR

Of course the Flying Scotsman is not the first train that has gone missing but we didn't want to alarm the public. You know what they're like.

MILLIGAN

I wish I did know what they like. Yes, I've got a photograph of the public here.

INSPECTOR
That's a remarkable likeness of them all.

MILLIGAN
Yes, you wait till I take it out of the envelope.

INSPECTOR
Well that envelope bears a remarkable likeness of them. Now, back to the train.

MILLIGAN
It's when I have my back to the train, that they're stolen.

INSPECTOR
We believe that somewhere in this country, there is a Bermuda triangle effect.

MILLIGAN
Well here is a triangle effect.

(SFX: TRIANGLE)

INSPECTOR
Sadly, they're completely different. We believe the trains are passing through this region, wherever it is, and vanishing. What on earth is happening?

MILLIGAN
I don't know inspector, but I suspect that the Railway trains at stations are vanishing.

INSPECTOR
That's it! How did you guess?

MILLIGAN
Well, after you told me, I put two and two together and made seven-million, five-hundred and-thirty-six.

INSPECTOR
That's near enough.

GRAMS

ANNOUNCER
And so, in a field near Carlisle by the railway line, stood a man in a ginger beard and a spotted jockstrap.

(SFX: FARMER APPROACHING, WHISTLING)

FARMER
Hello… who be ye?

MILLIGAN
I be Glasgow Central.

FARMER
Would you like to come and meet the wife?

MILLIGAN
Oh thank you.

(SFX: SQUEAKY DOOR OPEN.)

MILLIGAN
That's a funny sounding wife you've got…

FARMER
I'll have to give her a spot of oil. I'll just introduce you first. This is Glasgow central, my dear.

WIFE

Oh yes, come in. Like a cup of tea smashed over your head would you?

MILLIGAN

Thank you. I'd like that very much.

FARMER

I found this gentleman standing in one of our fields by the railway line. I thought I'd bring him home so he can live with us.

MILLIGAN

But I'm on secret government work.

FARMER

Couldn't you do it as a hobby?

MILLIGAN

Only in my spare time.

WIFE

Would you like a curry up your legs?

MILLIGAN

Oh thank you.

WIFE

Vindaloo?

MILLIGAN

Not while the train is standing in the station.

FARMER

So would you like to be one of the family then?

The Case of the Disappearing Flying Scotsman

MILLIGAN
Yes please. I'll be Uncle Glasgow Central.

WIFE
Tea-time, Uncle Glasgow Central. I've made five thousand corned beef sandwiches.

MILLIGAN
Thank you. I appreciate your lifetimes work and that appalling impression of a woman that you're doing. I'll write to the official secrets act and he can come and live with us too.

FARMER
As long as he don't tell no one else.

MILLIGAN
No, he clearly knows how to keep a secret, don't worry.

(SFX: TRAIN PULLING OUT OF STATION.)

ANNOUNCER
And so the Flying Scotsman disappeared into the Bermuda effect near Carlisle and about the same time the official secrets act went missing. The government were appalled and the upshot was that none other than the PM made a visit to an obscure farm near Carlisle.

(SFX: KNOCKING ON DOOR. DOOR CREAKS OPEN.)

MILLIGAN
Hello, I'm Uncle Glasgow Central.

CHURCHILL
Hello, I'm the Prime Minister. Could I possibly have a word with the official secrets act?

MILLIGAN

He's gone to bed with piles.

CHURCHILL

Oh well, just tell him not to tell anyone.

MILLIGAN

Tell him not to tell anyone what?

CHURCHILL

We don't know either—he's a secretive little brat!... Quiet, or we won't hear the end title music. Because we are not going to find out anything else, are we? Tonight? We can all go home—those of you who have homes to go to—the Government is still working on that one...

GRAMS—PLAY OUT, MUSIC IN STRONG

THE END

It went well! No scowls at the end! Audience OK, laughed often— but not carried away to another dimension! Nobody seemed to notice. Spike leaves like a plumber who has done a good job—cleared the blocked sink! Earned his fee, like the artisan he is—time to go home. On the way he signs a few autographs—careful calligraphy, beautiful handwriting...

Love, Light and Peace, Spike.

A good sign. Deep breaths, John. On to the next. Paul Spencer, producer, all smiles....

EPISODE 2
JONAH AND THE WHALE

Written by John Antrobus

Wow! Today so far—weird. Between read-through and recording ...

When I arrived Spike was on the piano, not a bad sign in itself, playing ' Laura ', a song he composed for his daughter. It is beautiful though too gothic nostalgic far away life is beautiful but not here, for my taste. So I could not read his mood from that. Nor in the read-through of the script. The rest of the cast found it amusing while Spike remained in neutral. As to cuts that he wanted, when I protested to one of them he said, what do I know? I bow to smaller minds. I only created the Goon Show and for doing so was crucified by the BBC... But he hasn't actually walked out, so...

On with the show!

ANNOUNCER

The BBC presents the Milligan papers written by John Antrobus.

GRAMS IN STRONG

ANNOUNCER

Episode 2—Jonah and the Whale. Our story opens, like most stories, in the Balham Labour Exchange.

ASSISTANT

Good morning.

MILLIGAN

Yes.

ASSISTANT
Can I take your name?

MILLIGAN
No. If you did that what would I use?

ASSISTANT
Name?

MILLIGAN
Very well. Jonah.

ASSISTANT
Occupation?

MILLIGAN
Prophet.

ASSISTANT
Occupation?

MILLIGAN
France.1944

ASSISTANT
Were you decorated?

MILLIGAN
Yes, but it's started to peel off.

ASSISTANT
Number of war medals.

MILLIGAN
Nil.

ASSISTANT
Tottenham Hotspur?

MILLIGAN
Three.

ASSISTANT
Would you be willing to travel to work?

MILLIGAN
Yes, as long as I don't get there.

ASSISTANT
Place of birth?

MILLIGAN
A tree.

ASSISTANT
Any special skills?

MILLIGAN
Well, I like getting a laugh… I can massage eggs without breaking them and standing on one leg in a bowl of custard while whistling 'Ave Maria' in Latvian, but of course there isn't much call for that type of work.

ASSISTANT
Yes, I'm not surprised, yes. Will you take any employment that is offered to you?

MILLIGAN
Could you rephrase that?

ASSISTANT
Yes. Is that employment any you that offered to take will?

MILLIGAN
Er, evasive answer.

ASSISTANT
So you've refuse to work!

MILLIGAN
On religious grounds.

ASSISTANT
Like what?

MILLIGAN
Erm, cemeteries.

ASSISTANT
You refuse to work on religious grounds like a cemetery?

MILLIGAN
Yes, I have a morbid fear of drowning.

ASSISTANT
Most cemeteries are inland.

MILLIGAN
Yes, that makes it more difficult for the lifeboats to get to me.

ASSISTANT
You could be buried at sea.

MILLIGAN
That would create a splash!

ASSISTANT
Would you describe yourself as incorrigible?

MILLIGAN
Well alright, "I am incorrigible."

ASSISTANT
I'm finished with you.

MILLIGAN
Darling...

(SFX: BUZZER.)

ASSISTANT
Security. Please remove that man. Get him out of here. Quick.

MILLIGAN
Thank you! Thank you you for laying hands on mr and throwing me into the stree.

(SFX: DOOR slams.)

(SFX: CAR HORN, SWERVE, CRASH. MILLIGAN scream.)

MILLIGAN
Thank you for knocking me down. It was my fault for standing on the pavement. A prophet is without honour in his own country, that is how it should be. He should expect to be knocked down every 2 minutes...

(SFX: CAR HORN, SWERVE, CRASH. MILLIGAN scream.)

MILLIGAN
You're early. That was ninety seconds...

ANNOUNCER
Shortly afterwards, Jonah made haste to a local tobacconists.

(SFX: SHOP DOOR BELL.)

MILLIGAN

Two ounces of shag please. (Aside) I think there's a touch of the double entendre in that…

SHOP ASSISTANT

Certainly. Wait a minute… aren't you one Jonah?

MILLIGAN

Yes, I counted me this morning and I came to a total of one Jonah.

SHOP ASSISTANT

Don't you recognise me, Jonah? I am God.

MILLIGAN

Good God! What are you doing running a tobacconists?

SHOP ASSISTANT

Well, I had to use my redundancy money for something.

MILLIGAN

Here, I used to see you preaching in the parks. You're the God of Balham, aren't you?

SHOP ASSISTANT

That is correct, you're right, my dear man. And soon the world.

MILLIGAN

You used to have terrible arguments with the God of Tooting, didn't you?

SHOP ASSISTANT

Right. Right. I didn't like his dog much.

MILLIGAN

I remember. His dog bit you and died of food poisoning. Do you still do the walking on the water?

SHOP ASSISTANT

No, I don't walk anywhere much these days. I'm too tired.

(SFX: CASH REGISTER.)

MILLIGAN

I find you hard to believe.

SHOP ASSISTANT

What, man? That I am God of all the world?

MILLIGAN

No, for charging me £12.30 for two ounces of shag.

SHOP ASSISTANT

Look I'll throw in a box of liquorice all-sorts if you'll be my prophet, Jonah. In return, I shall have your complete obedience for the rest of your life.

MILLIGAN

Hmm, those hours sound a bit long. Would you throw in another couple of ounces of shag?

SHOP ASSISTANT

Yes, Jonah. All that I have is yours.

MILLIGAN

I'll take the Evening News as well, then.

(SFX: CASH REGISTER.)

SHOP ASSISTANT

Paper-being-handed-across-acting. Anything else?

MILLIGAN

No, I'm satisfied, God. What do you want me to do then? Look after the shop?

SHOP ASSISTANT

No, no, Jonah. I shall appear unto you in the fullness of time in a Burning Bush.

MILLIGAN

Holy Smokes!

GRAMS

ANNOUNCER

And so did Jonah continue for many a day, visiting God in his tobacconists, and taking from there shag, liquorice and the evening papers. Verily, he did take these and much more from God, and never once did God complain, or even put them on the slate. No, all things were given to Jonah, his beloved. Then, one day, God did appear to Jonah as he had promised so to do. And God did shout through his letterbox:

SHOP ASSISTANT

Jonah! Get thee to Nineveh, and cry out against that wicked city!

ANNOUNCER

Jonah was troubled for he did not expect God to shout through his letterbox—and he knew not of Nineveh, and he did straight away consult with an atlas.

ATLAS MAN
So you want to build up your strength do you?

MILLIGAN
Yes, I've stopped doing it.

ATLAS MAN
I'm glad to hear. Tell me, Jonah, you're ashamed are you, when you stand in front of the mirror and flex your muscles.

MILLIGAN
No, I'm just ashamed when I stand in front of the mirror.

ATLAS MAN
Ah.

MILLIGAN
I daren't lay down, they'd bury me.

ATLAS MAN
What happens when you put your bathing trunks on?

MILLIGAN
They fall down. I get arrested for mini-flashing.

ATLAS
Do you work out?

MILLIGAN
Please don't use the word work. It frightens me.

ATLAS MAN
Did you bring your cheque book with you?

MILLIGAN
No, I'm too weak to carry it.

ATLAS MAN

No money?

MILLIGAN

Oh money... Money is too heavy for me. I get a financial rupture.

ATLAS MAN

What's that?

MILLIGAN

A lump sum.

ATLAS MAN

How did you plan to pay for this miraculous bodybuilding course?

MILLIGAN

By entering for the alternative Miss Third World Competition and winning a candlelit supper for two with Piers Morgan..

(SFX: WINDOW SMASH.)

MILLIGAN

Thank you for throwing me out the window during that laugh. It was truly a shattering experience.

ANNOUNCER

At home, Jonah met with yet more discouragement.

MILLIGAN

Thank you for that discouraging announcement. Oh, hello dear.

WIFE

Nineveh? No one goes to Nineveh. It's a dump. My sister got molested there.

MILLIGAN
Only if they pay her ten pound an hour.

WIFE
That's because of the inflation.

MILLIGAN
Yes, well she had it done, didn't she?

WIFE
Never mind my sister, the Harris's went to Nineveh for a fortnight last year. The gran-ma got Montezuma's Revenge—the mother got Delhi Belly—then the son got the Bombay Trots!

MILLIGAN
You mean?

WIFE
Runs in the family!

MILLIGAN
I shall cry out against the Montezuma's Revenge in Nineveh. I shall say "The Montezuma's Revenge's are upon you! Repent! Repent! Repent!"

(SFX: RASPBERRY.)

ANNOUNCER
But great fear did come upon Jonah and he did not depart hence to Nineveh. Instead, Jonah, feeling the Wrath of God, decided to leave Balham. And feeling the wrath of his wife, he left her too. And he went hence to the port of Jodhpur to seek a passage to Tarshish.

(SFX: SHIP FOGHORN.)

OMNES
Anchors away / ahoy, ahoy! etc.

CAPTAIN
Batten the hatches!

SAILOR 1
Aye, aye, sir!

CAPTAIN
Loosen your mainstays!

SAILOR 2
Aye, aye, sir!

SAILOR 1
Ooh, that's better, dear!

CAPTAIN
Coming up one of the mooring ropes, I—Capt'n of this ship—spied a stranger climbing aboard.

MILLIGAN
Hello sailor. Is this the way to the first class cabins?

CAPTAIN
Why?

MILLIGAN
I'm a first-class stowaway.

(MILLIGAN screams. SFX: SPLASH.)

MILLIGAN
Thank you for throwing me off your ship into a shark-infested quayside, Captain.

CAPTAIN

Here, one moment… is that not a ticket in your hat, lad. Give it here! It's for for a journey to Tarsish, paid for by the Balham Social Security?

MILLIGAN

Oh! I'd forgotten about that.

CAPTAIN

Well Jonah, this entitles you to work your passage. As do the prunes you had for breakfast.

MILLIGAN

I made sure he had that line. I have been betrayed by the Balham Social Security Office.

CAPTAIN

Right you lubber, get below. Cast off forward! Cast off aft!

MILLIGAN

What's that supposed to mean?

CAPTAIN

I don't know. I got it from a knitting pattern.

SAILOR

Oh, he makes lovely pullovers! Bonar, bonar!

(SFX: SHIP BELL.)

CAPTAIN

Right ! All hands on deck! Call the roll, busom!

BOSUN (Deep voice)

Busom?

CAPTAIN

(Corrects himself) Bosun.

BOSUN

That's better. That's the last free tattoo he's getting—of a dragon disappearing up his...

CAPTAIN

Call the roll!

SAILOR 1

Cut-throat Crossbones! I'm the ships mate.

MILLIGAN

Jonah! I'm the cooks mate.

SAILOR

Able seaman Wilomena Trubshaw! I'm everybody's mate!

CAPTAIN

Just a minute! I don't allow no women on me deck. I thought you was the cabin boy.

SAILOR

I was until when we went ashore in Cairo where I met an obliging surgeon—and the rest is history.

CAPTAIN

Right! Weigh anchor! Weigh the anchor!

MILLIGAN

Five hundred weight!

CAPTAIN

That's a good guess. You win the prize this week.

SFX. SHIPS BELL.

ANNOUNCER
The gangway was pulled in and the ship sailed from Portsmouth harbour.

MILLIGAN
Well done, Captain.

CAPTAIN
Yes, I am a well done captain. Thank-ee, Jonah. But we did forget one thing.

MILLIGAN
Yes, to go aboard.

ANNOUNCER
As they stood waiting for a laugh, the Captain and Jonah repaired to a dockside caff, where they repaired a dockside caff. Soon they had a flourishing business, repairing dockside caffs. One evening, a stranger came to them, as they caroused.

(SFX: TAPPING OF BLIND STICK.)

OLD BLIND PEW
Are you leading me right, Jim lad?

JIM
Yes, come on Blind Pew.? This way. This way...

OLD BLIND PEW
Give me your hand, Jim lad.

JIM
Ow! That's not it!

OLD BLIND PEW
Oh, sorry…

JIM
Come on, Pew!

OLD BLIND PEW
All right.

(OLD BLIND PEW screams. SFX: WATER SPLASH.)

ANNOUNCER
That night, after Jim Hawkins had dried out Old Blind Pew by hanging him on a line…

MILLIGAN
You need a better line than that for a laugh.

ANNOUNCER
Thank you. The intrepid couple made their way to the repaired caff. Where they met…

OLD BLIND PEW
Aha! Jonah! Give me your hand. Jonah? Where be ye, man ? Man or beast?

MILLIGAN
Here I be, Blind Pew—waiting for my cue when you have stopped improvising.

OLD BLIND PEW
Oh! You startled me. Here? Where is thee? Let us shake hands on this meeting.

MILLIGAN

Ow!! Blind Pew has given me the Black Spot. Am I doomed?

OLD BLIND PEW

The same doom that drove me blind!

(OLD BLIND PEW laughs wickedly. SFX: LIGHTNING CLAP.)

MILLIGAN

Listen, Blind Pew, in the giving me of the Black Spot, have you eternally Damned me?

OLD BLIND PEW

I don't know. I'm just looking for a good night out, sunshine. I'm sorry, you took it the wrong way. You meet some funny people don't you, around here.

MILLIGAN

Not on this show, you don't. Listen, what does the black spot mean, Blind Pew?

OLD BLIND PEW

It don't mean nothing, it's just a bit of black cardboard.

MILLIGAN

Oh, then why did you give it to me?

OLD BLIND PEW

Look matey, if you can't take a bit of black cardboard in the right spirit, that's not my concern. I like good company! I'm going somewhere else

MILLIGAN

This is somewhere else.

BLIND PEW

It is when you are somewhere else, matey. But until you get there this place is here!

MILLIGAN

Well go and stand over there and then here will be somewhere else.

BLIND PEW

Only as far as I am concerned. Why are you getting philosophical?

MILLIGAN

Because I'm wearing bicycle clips. Goodnight

SFX: DOOR OPENS, BLIND STICK TAPPING.)

ANNOUNCER

And so Blind Pew disappeared into the night, seeking more entertainment. He found it with George Chisholm and his Gentlemen of Jazz.

GEORGE CHISHOLM MUSICAL INTERLUDE.

ANNOUNCER

And Jonah, fearing the Wrath of God, took passage on a ship bound for Tarsish.

(SFX: STORM.)

CAPTAIN

And a mighty storm overtook the ship, so that the crew, having prayed to no avail and in fear for their souls sought out Jonah who lay asleep in the hold. (aside) My throat hurts.

MILLIGAN

(SNORES) Zed-zed-zed-zed-zed-zed. (SNORES) Zed-zed-zed-zed-zed-zed.

CAPTAIN
Wake up Jonah, we've thrown all your Z's overboard to lighten our vessel yet still we are in danger of floundering.

MILLIGAN
Well, throw the ship overboard as well.

SAILOR
Look sailor, we've got a full Force 10 out there. No messing. I've laddered three pairs of tights already so get praying.

MILLIGAN
I'm not going to pray for three pairs of laddered tights. Oh I don't know though… God is angry with me because I will not go to Nineveh.

SAILOR
I got the runs in Nineveh. It really hit the fan.

CAPTAIN
This storm could be God's vengeance on you, Jonah. You're bringing us bad luck, admit it! You are a Jonah, Jonah!

MILLIGAN
Yes, I am a Jonah hyphen Jonah-Jonah. It's hereditary, you see, it's in the blood. In fact, wait for this, I'm a blood Jonah! Thank you. Take me out and throw me overboard so that the wrath of God will be appeased and the storm shall cease.

CAPTAIN
Aye!

CAPTAIN & SAILOR
One—two—three!

(MILLIGAN SCREAMS. SFX: SPLASH)

MILLIGAN
It's worked!... Help!

ANNOUNCER
And the crew pulled Jonah back aboard.

CAPTAIN
Throw him back again.

(MILLIGAN SCREAMS. SFX: SPLASH)

ANNOUNCER
In the instant of the storm's decease, a mighty humpback whale swallowed Jonah whole and carried him to the bottom of the ocean. Where he had ab extraordinary encounter...

(SFX: CAVERNOUS PIT. DRIPPING WATER ETC.)

MILLIGAN
Establishing BBC effects—inside a whale.

MATE
Hello? Hello, mate! Hello?

MILLIGAN
Hello mate. What are you doing in here? Are you the extraordinary encounter?

MATE
Yes, mate. And, believe it or not, mate, I massage eggs without breaking them standing on one leg in a bowl of custard while whistling 'Ave Maria' in Latvian.

MILLIGAN
I thought there wasn't much call for that kind of work.

MATE
There isn't.

MILLIGAN
Nor that kind of line apparently. That's why I gave it to you in the read-through.

MATE
Thanks, mate.

SFX RUMBLING NOISE ECHOES.

MILLIGAN
Here, what's that noise?

MATE
That's Moby Dick.

MILLIGAN
That must be painful. I don't want to move too far down . His stomach might get knotted.

MATE
Get knotted?

MILLIGAN
There's no need to be insulting. Just cos you've ben down here so long.

MATE
I've been in here for nigh on twenty years, mate. He swallowed me whole.

MILLIGAN

I'm glad somebody did Nobody else would take you seriously.

MATE

Mate, Moby always gets bad digestion... He gets nervous when the whaling ships come near.

MILLIGAN

Can't he take anything for it?

MATE

Yes, the Red Sea three times a day, mate. You get a good sluicing! Oh, listen to that, mate! Moby's got the Montezumases bad this time.

SFX MORE RUMBLING,

MILLIGAN

No, that was me that time.

MATE

Oh! Don't come too close, mate.

MILLIGAN

I can't get away from it. Here, how did you come to be inside Moby Dick?

MATE

Well, I got rehoused by the council, mate. Foolishly I said I wanted to live in Wales ... I had a terrible place before.

MILLIGAN

Plaice? There can't be much room inside a plaice, mate?

MATE

No, it was more of a flat, mate.

MILLIGAN
A plaice is a flat fish.

MATE
I know mate. They promised me a bigger three-bedroomed fish…

MILLIGAN
I think we've gone as far as we can with this conversation.

(SFX: ANNOUNCEMENT BELL.)

ANNOUNCER
Attention please, we are currently cruising at a depth of seventeen fathoms and will shortly be surfacing for air. We trust you have obtained all your purchases from the duty-free shop and that you will consider travelling by whale again. Thank you.

MILLIGAN
Who's that? Making that announcement?

MATE
Captain Aheb. Moby's hired him.

MILLIGAN
He's lucky. He couldn't get a job anywhere else acting like that.

(SFX: SONAR NOISE.)

MATE
Oh mate! We're going up! Standby to regurgitate!

MILLIGAN
I'm sick of this!

(SFX: CLUNK!)

MATE
Oh mate! It's the depth charges.

MILLIGAN
Thank God, I thought it was you.

MATE
It's the Ruskie whalers.

MILLIGAN
They've got it, as well.

ANNOUNCER
Standby to crash dive! Standby to crash dive!

(SFX: WARNING SIREN.)

MILLIGAN
Oh this is terrible! Why don't they leave the whales alone?

MATE
A loan, mate? What would a whale do with a loan?

(SFX: EXPLOSION)

ANNOUNCER
The Russian fleet forced Moby to the surface and mercilessly killed him. They hauled the beautiful creature out of the sea and set to work on processing it. Sometime later, in a supermarket in Kilburn, a woman returned a tin of cat food and complained to the manager.

WOMAN
I can hear something inside.

SHOP SELLER
I beg your pardon, madam?

WOMAN
Here, you listen to it.

(SFX: WHALE CALL.)

MILLIGAN (muffled)
Can you hear me? This is Jonah! I'm a prophet! You can't do this to me!

SHOP SELLER
This is the new, talking, cat food, madam.

WOMAN
Oh, that's nice.

MILLIGAN
Open this bleeding tin!

SHOP SELLER
Please, moderate your language in that tin! We have a consumer out here.

MILLIGAN
We have a consumer in here!

WOMAN
Come on, into my shopping bag you go...

MILLIGAN
What is your name?

WOMAN
Mrs T.

MILLIGAN

Mrs. Thalidomide, I don't wish to abuse your hospitality.

WOMAN

You haven't seen it yet.

MILLIGAN

You haven't seen mine!

GRAMS

ANNOUNCER

And so Mrs Thalidomide took the defected tin of cat food tin home and opened it. She instantly fell in love with Jonah and promptly got rid of her cat. This may have provided a happy ending to our tale, but for the Wrath of God, who was still annoyed with Jonah taking so much from his tobacconists. Anyway, the upshot was that one night a call came through the letterbox at Mrs. Thalidomide's residence.

GOD

Jonah! Get thee to Nineveh and cry out against that wicked city.

THROAT

Who's that out there?

WOMAN

Go back to sleep, Frederick.

THROAT

All right.

MILLIGAN

Who's Frederick? Never mind... Yes God, I will go to Nineveh and cry out against that wicked city.

GRAMS

ANNOUNCER
And thus, Jonah went to Nineveh at last and did cry out against that wicked city, calling them to repentance.

(SFX: RASPBERRY.)

OMNES
(Wailing)

MILLIGAN
Repent!

(SFX: RASPBERRY.)

OMNES
(Wailing)

MILLIGAN
Repent!

SCOTSMAN
'Ere, just a minute, 'scuse me, why do you keep on saying repent?

MILLIGAN
It's a repeat for those who didn't hear it the first time. Are you a Ninevite?

SCOTSMAN
Nah, Jimmie, I'm from Aberdeen.

MILLIGAN
We can still be friends.

SCOTSMAN

We tried Torremolinos last year, didn't we hen?

(SFX: CHICKEN CLUCKING)

SCOTSMAN

Aye, but we got the runs. The chicken runs. So we decided to try Nineveh this year.

(SFX: RASPBERRIES)

OMNES

Oh woe, woe! / Not again! / No more curried egg for me etc etc.

ANNOUNCER

And so, in conclusion, God sent Montezuma's Revenge to Jonah in Nineveh. Fortunately before I was stricken myself, I was able to cry out to George Chisholm—take it away, lads!

GRAMS IN STRONG

THE END.

Incredible! It worked! Spike started slowly but saw that the audience was catching on and loving it... So he went full throttle and gave us wonderful energy as did all the cast (including me,) it was easy, coming off an audience laughing like drains!!

Spike even came up to me and said, We've got a hit! I should have taken his words down and got him to sign! Anyway this week is not next week....

EPISODE 3
FROM RAGS TO MORE RAGS

Written by John Antrobus

A few desperate words before the execution. Spike was already here when I arrived apparently composing a funeral dirge on the piano. The piano should be locked up and so should Spike. My smile and cheerful hello Spike bounced off his stony features... the show is nothing without him that's why it's called The Milligan Papers. Everything alright at home, I asked, stupidly. I don't have a home, it's occupied by idiots. I'm living in my office, his words dropped onto the carpet, staining it. He looked like he lived in his office. Unshaven. Van Gogh haunted. He paints like Van Gogh. I checked, he still had both ears so one wasn't in the post...

John, he nodded, this isn't going to work.

It's up to us, Spike.

No, he said. The best days have gone and they were terrible enough...

Then the read through... like pouring energy into a black hole in space. At least Spike was indifferent to cutting the script into another shape this week. Even the determined Spike pleasing keep the ship afloat producer, Paul Spencer, looked desolate...

Good luck in your next job, Spike told him.

The audience are coming in. They look happy enough. Perhaps their energy will rescue us...

I don't know. I don't know. I DON'T KNOW!! Bring it on....

ANNOUNCER
The BBC presents The Milligan Papers written by John Antrobus.

GRAMS IN STRONG

(SFX: RUDIMENTAL STRUMMING ON GUITAR)

BEGGAR
"Who Wants to Be a Millionaire? I don't."

(SFX—PENNY RATTLE IN CAN)

BEGGAR
Oh, thank you, sir. God bless you, sir.

MAN
That's alright, unemployed fellow.

BEGGAR
Just one moment, sir. Excuse me, but it's a fake.

MAN
What?

BEGGAR
A counterfeit, sir. Go on, bite it, that's the way to tell.

MAN
Hmm. Yes, you're right, by Jove.

BEGGAR
I hope you don't mind my mentioning it, sir.

MAN
Not all. After all, it's not every day one comes across a counterfeit tin cup.

GRAMS

ANNOUNCER
We present "From Rags to More Rags"—a desperate tale of a young man's search for fame, fortune and a social disease. Our story begins on the estate of Lord Glazing-Glazing, better known to his friends as Double-Glazing.

MILLIGAN
He's terrible at lying.

ANNOUNCER
Oh?

MILLIGAN
You can see right through him! Even with the double glazing.

(GRAMS – CORNY GAG)

LORD (calling)
Spong! Spong!

MILLIGAN / OLD BUTLER
Ah, yes, yes sir.

Spong, the butler, practises grovelling...

LORD
I have a question.

MILLIGAN
Pickled cocoanut, sir.

LORD
That isn't the answer.

MILLIGAN / OLD BUTLER
I'll try harder next time, sir.

LORD

My question is, what is it like to be poor?

MILLIGAN / OLD BUTLER

Oh, it's horrible, sir. Horrible.

LORD

You mean, it's not at all like being very rich? Like being the richest man in England?

MILLIGAN / OLD BUTLER

No, sir. It's just the opposite, sir.

LORD

Let me work that out. You mean, it's like being me but without any money?

MILLIGAN / OLD BUTLER

No, it's like being me but without any money.

LORD

Oh dear, that must be dreadful.

MILLIGAN / OLD BUTLER

Yes, sir.

LORD

Being very, very poor like you, fascinates me.

MILLIGAN / OLD BUTLER

Yes, it is fascinating, sir. Only the other day, I said to my wife "how fascinating it is to be very, very poor, darling." And then she said to me…

LORD

Yes, what did you say to you?

MILLIGAN / OLD BUTLER

She said "goodbye."

LORD

Fascinating.

MILLIGAN / OLD BUTLER

It's very fascinating.

LORD

Right, pack my toothbrush and five hundred million pounds.

MILLIGAN / OLD BUTLER

Yes, sir. Do you want some spending money as well, sir?

LORD

Yes, three buckets full.

MILLIGAN / OLD BUTLER

I'll just empty the socks out, sir. Phew! What a scorcher!

LORD

I'm going to find the poorest man in England and change places with him.

MILLIGAN / OLD BUTLER

Look no farther, sir. And to prove it, here is my birth certificate.

LORD

My goodness, you're right. Look – no further.

LORD

No, not you, Spong. You've got a roof over your head, haven't you?

MILLIGAN / OLD BUTLER

No, no. My cottage has not got a roof over my head, sir.

LORD

Well, when that cottage is finished, you will have.

MILLIGAN / OLD BUTLER

That cottage has been finished for years, sir, like me. Will you be needing the po again tonight, sir?

LORD

What I don't understand about you, Spong, is why you don't join the Communist Party, and rise up against us landed gentry and murder us all in our beds.

MILLIGAN / OLD BUTLER

Well sir, the answer to that is simple. Me.

LORD

You're the answer?

MILLIGAN / OLD BUTLER

Yes, sir, and I'm simple, too. You see, we'd have to make the beds afterwards… All those stains. Don't think of that, do you? All you think about is being murdered in your beds. But who has to clear up the mess and empty the buckets? We do, sir! We have to get the trams running again, Me Lord. The ones we turned over to make the barricades with—no wonder we're all late for work.

LORD

Yes, yes, I suppose so, Spong. Go on then, let's find the poorest man in Britain. Let's get up to town. Good chance of finding him up there, wouldn't you say?

MILLIGAN / OLD BUTLER

Yes, sir. One moment, sir?

LORD
Oh?

MILLIGAN / OLD BUTLER
You're not hatching a plot to exchange places with such a poor wretch, are you? And leave me unemployed?

LORD

Yes I am, Spong. I'm sick and tired of being rich, you hear? I want to know what it's like to touch the depths of despair. To have my trousers frayed at the bottom...

MILLIGAN / OLD BUTLER

I can do that now, sir, hang on....

LORD

To be underneath the arches throwing a dead rat at another derelict alcoholic!

MILLIGAN / OLD BUTLER

I can get you a dead rat, sir. I always keep one handy. You never know when you'll need a dead rat—not in my line of business.. Oh dear, sir, if you go through with this where's me pound a year going to come from?

LORD

You're just thinking about yourself, aren't you, eh? Spong. You should be ashamed of yourself.

MILLIGAN / OLD BUTLER

I am, sir. Deeply ashamed.

LORD

Good. Well done!

MILLIGAN / OLD BUTLER

But I cannot keep myself in a state of ashamed, sir, for less than £1 a year. My lord, when you find this poor wretch you are looking for—how long were you thinking of exchanging places with him, sir?

LORD (much deliberation)

Well, er... how about... fifteen....

MILLIGAN / OLD BUTLER
Weeks.

LORD
Minutes? I don't think I could take much more than that. That should be lesson enough for me.

MILLIGAN / OLD BUTLER
Well, come on then, me Lord. Let's get going...

(GRAMS)

ANNOUNCER
Little did Lord Glazing-Glazing realise that he was in fact of poor lineage. He'd been born of desperately poor tenant farmers on his own estate and exchanged while in the cradle by the mad evolutionary scientist, Terence Wacky.

WACKY
(Insane, manic laughing)

ANNOUNCER
Thank you, that's enough. Wacky was incarcerated in a mental asylum for predicting the coming of the motorcar. Unfortunately, he predicted it too late, and it hit him.

WACKY
Beep.... Er, beep.... No.... Beep, beep. Beep-beep-be...no (etc)

MILLIGAN
Good luck in your next job.

MILLIGAN / GERMAN DOCTOR
Oh, you are very interesting. What is with the making of all this 'beep-beep'?

WACKY
(Manic laughing)

ANNOUNCER
Yes, that's enough, thank you… (WACKY continues giggling) Enough!

WACKY
Could you do a mad laugh like that? If you think it's that easy, could you do one? As an announcer?

ANNOUNCER
Of course I can.

(WACKY and ANNOUNCER amuse each other with their mad laughing.)

(GRAMS)

(SFX: FARM YARD – (ANIMAL NOISES FROM THE CAST))

MILLIGAN / FAR (WEST-COUNTRY ACCENT)
While yon announcer joins mad revolutionary scientist Wacky in the jigsaw factory, things were taking a very strange turn on Dung Farm, which is why all the cast is making them animal noises. And very nice they are, too. Tom Dung is son of Farmer Dung, who is me speaking. He was not really my son. He had been exchanged at birth for a wardrobe and a chamber-pot which came in very useful. I used to keep it under the bed for emergencies, but after a fortnight, I soon had it filled. It was then I knew I'd need a bigger wardrobe… He had in fact being born of Lady Draft-Excluder, known to her friends as Lady Double-Glazing. We find Tom down in the pig pen.

(SFX: CHICKENS.)

MILLIGAN / FARMER
No, no, no! Tom down in the pig pen.

OMNES
Oh sorry etc.

(SFX: PIGS.)

TOM DUNG
Well, here I am down in the pig pen. It don't feel right. I keep blushing when I look at pigs. Except Bessie here, who I know better than the others. Good girl. Oh you know, ever since father married again, I felt like an intruder.

MILLIGAN / FARMER
I'll try and get you one, lad.

TOM DUNG
I know Dad did right to advertise in the Mariners Weekly for a new bride, and I can't say I find anything particularly wrong with leading stoker Sam Groin, retired. But I'm dashed if I'll call him mother. I bet they're talking about me now; that's why I'm blushing. All nice and cosy round the kitchen fire while I'm doing the mucking out.

MILLIGAN / FARMER
All right, Sam.

SAM (OLD SEA DOG)
Aha, aye, yah. Ahoy to starboard and hankle the winkie-bloaters.

MILLIGAN / FARMER
I'm very worried about our Tom, mother.

SAM
Oh arr.

MILLIGAN / FARMER
I'm worried about you as well. Your acting in particular like.

SAM
Nothing that a good keyhole hollering won't put right, and a 'ha-harrr'.

MILLIGAN / FARMER

I daresay you're right with you 'ha-harrs.'

SAM

Arrr!

MILLIGAN / FARMER

Are you enjoying smoking those curtains?

SAM

Well, I'm all out of carpet.

MILLIGAN / FARMER

It's good stuff.

TOM DUNG

Father! Mother! Father, mother, pay attention. I can't take it anymore.

MILLIGAN / FARMER

I told you, those enemas were upsetting the balance of his mind, Sam.

TOM DUNG

No, it's not the enemas. It's the feeling that I don't belong here. I'm going up London.

MILLIGAN / FARMER

He's going up London. Did you hear that, Sam? He's going up London.

SAM

I heard "up Wolverhampton."

TOM DUNG

Then I'll go up Wolverhampton and then go up London.

(GRAMS—DRAMATIC CHORD)

ANNOUNCER
I'd like to point out at this stage that my position in this story has become quite untenable. I'm only here to do the linking announcements. I only come in just before the show starts to have a cup of tea with the cast and to talk about the days racing at Newbury, that sort of thing.

OMNES
Arrr!

ANNOUNCER
And now here I am in a locked ward with Terence Wacky, the mad evolutionary scientist.

WACKY
(manic laughing)

ANNOUNCER
Stop it! You'll go blind. If some kind listener would inform the BBC that I'm being held here against my will, I'd be very grateful.

MILLIGAN / GERMAN DOCTOR
Ah, zat is very interesting. Zo you have ze delusions that you are ze director general of ze BBC?

ANNOUNCER
No, I'm an announcer.

MILLIGAN / GERMAN DOCTOR
Ah, zis week an announcer, next week a director general, und soon, ze vorld!

ANNOUNCER
I do sometimes get the awful feeling, doctor, that I'm the scottish George Chisholm and His Gentlemen of the Jazz.

MILLIGAN / GERMAN DOCTOR
Hmm. Did you hear any muzic?

ANNOUNCER
No, I wouldn't describe it that way.

MILLIGAN / GERMAN DOCTOR
Oh?

ANNOUNCER
It's more like this...

GEORGE CHISHOLM INTERLUDE

(SFX—HORSE-DRAWN CARRIAGE)

LORD
Stop here, driver.

DRIVER
Woah! Woah! Here, this sound effects out of control, sir.

(SFX—HORSE NEIGH)

LORD
Blast the BBC sound library! Woah!

(GRAMS—MARCH BAND MUSIC)

LORD
Stop that Brigade of guards! Woah!

DRIVER

Halt!

LORD

Driver, see that all the men are fed and watered.

DRIVER

What time will you be needing the Brigade of guards again, sir?

LORD

At quack o'clock.

DRIVER

Quack o'clock? Right sir. I'll set my duck for the right time.

LORD

Is that a Greenwich Mean Duck?

DRIVER

It is, sir.

LORD

You don't see a lot of them about.

DRIVER

About what, sir?

LORD

About quack o'clock.

DRIVER

Right, sir.

LORD

So-saying, I walked into my club.

(SFX—DOOR OPEN. BROTHEL SOUNDSCAPE. DOOR CLOSE.)

LORD

I thought I was walking into my club. My club was next door.

(SFX—DOOR OPEN. GENTLEMEN'S CLUB SOUNDSCAPE.)

BOOFY

Hello, Double-Glazing!

LORD

Hello, Boofy!

BOOFY

Care for a drink, would you?

LORD

Boofy, you might be wondering what I'm doing in town.

BOOFY

Well, if it's the usual, I wouldn't like to see your laundry bill.

LORD

No, no. You see, I'm here because I'm dissatisfied with the way I'm living.

BOOFY

Are you?

LORD

Yes, I want to find the poorest man in Britain and change places with him.

BOOFY

Well, I'm down to my last million?

LORD
Well, that doesn't make you the poorest man in Britain.

BOOFY
Doesn't it? You sure?

LORD
There are lots and lots of people out there on the streets this very day, Boofy, who are worth less than a million pounds.

BOOFY
Good God, how awful… no wonder they dress so badly. My God, look at the time! It's cluck-cluck!

LORD
I think your chicken's a little fast.

BOOFY
Yes, probably wrong to curry it. Still, I love a vindaloo.

LORD
Well, you could have trouble with the family there.

BOOFY
Oh, hers or mine?

LORD
Er, well, I was thinking of mine.

BOOFY
Yes, you always do, you're so selfish.

LORD
Excuse me Boofy, just a moment while I announce this next scene.

BOOFY
Well, if that's your attitude, I'll go and climb a mountain.

(SFX—DIZZY, WINDY HEIGHTS. BLIZZARD ETC.)

LORD
Boofy! Where are you??

BOOFY
It's a funny thing, I'm dangling off the top of Mount Everest.

LORD
Hang on!

BOOFY
The thought had occurred to me to hang on, yes

LORD
And now, dear listeners, owing to the indisposition of the announcer, it falls to me to say now we find two very poor men in a cardboard box under the arches at Charing Cross. Thank you. (calling) Boofy! Boofy!

BOOFY (calling)
Over here, Double-Glazing! Did you bring the Sherpas?

LORD
No. Only the Ovaltine and the appliance.

MATE
Oh, mate, have you got the cardboard box?

MATE'S MATE
I caught the cardboard box in Cairo.

MATE

I knew her well.

MATE'S MATE

Yes, mate. We should be inside it at Charing Cross, not halfway up a bleedin' mountain.

MATE

Yeah, we didn't get the proper introduction, mate.

MATE'S MATE

We're well-drawn working class cameos.

MATE

That's right, mate. Now that bleedin' announcers gone in a nuthouse with Terence Wacky the mad evolutionary scientist.

WACKY

(Manic laughing)

(SFX—WOODBLOCK)

WACKY

Ow!

MATE

Here, that blow on the nut to Terence Wacky has stopped the blizzard.

WACKY

Yes, you noticed? That's because it's all happening inside my head, you see. Hahahah! And another! Hahahah!

(SFX—WOODBLOCK)

WACKY
Ow!

ANNOUNCER
Quiet! For God's sake, there are other patients here trying to get some sleep!

MATE'S MATE
Mate, we're in the cardboard box now.

MATE
Yeah, but don't you give the credit to Terence Wacky, will you.

MATE'S MATE
No, mate. I won't give the credit to Terence Wacky.

MATE
Being inside his head, mate, would pose all sorts of philosophical questions that we're in-equipped to answer.

MATE'S MATE
Ah, mate here, you think we're written by Waiting for Beckett? He's very good, in't he?

MATE
Nah, mate. If we'd been written by Waiting for Blackett, we could do this in French. Comprendre?

MATE'S MATE
Mais certainement.

MATE
Certainement... Oui, oui (PRONOUNCED "OO-I, "OO-I"). Here, have a look outside.

MATE'S MATE
Outside what?

MATE
Outside the cardboard box, you twit!

MATE'S MATE
Yeah, alright.

(SFX—SQUEAKY DOOR OPENING)

MATE'S MATE
It's gorn!

MATE
Gorn? What's gorn?

MATE'S MATE
Outside! Outside is gorn!

MATE
That's very philosophical, that is, you know. Outside is gorn!

MATE'S MATE
Yeah, well, I think we should be rewritten.

MATE
Oh, what as?

MATE'S MATE
As, as philosophers.

MATE
Oh no. You have to start as a philosopher's mate first, mate.

MATE'S MATE
What? Holding all the tools?

MATE
Well, if you put it that way...

MATE'S MATE
Here, here, you mean that wouldn't even let us unblock a kharzi to start with, on our own?

MATE
No, that's too philosophical.

MATE'S MATE
Oooh!

MATE
Unblocking the kharzi? Who do you think you are? Socrates?

MATE'S MATE
Well, what about clearing the gutter of leaves? Could we do that in our first year?

MATE
Listen, mate, I ain't been to h'Oxford. It's no good asking me.

(SFX—DOORBELL)

LORD
Hello? Lord Double-Glazing here. Anyone in this humble cardboard box?

MATE
Here, where are you, sir?

LORD
Outside.

MATE

There is no outside.

LORD

Well, I brought some with me. I knew you were in stricken circumstances.

MATE

oh, I wondered what the pain was.

(SFX—DOOR OPENS)

MATE

Here, this isn't Charing Cross.

MATE'S MATE

What's outside, mate?

MATE

It's the Himalayas.

LORD

Look here, beggars can't be choosers.

MATE

Oh yes we can, mate. We chose this box. Harrods cardboard box this, in't it, mate.

MATE'S MATE

Yes, mate.

LORD

Really? How interesting. What was in it originally?

MATE & MATE'S MATE

We were.

LORD

But it says here on the box "one upright piano".

MATE

Yeah, but when you get it home and you unpack it, your upright piano, and say you want it moved across the room, then Harrods puts in a couple of delivery men so they can do it for you.

LORD

Then why aren't you with the piano?

MATE

Well, when they took the piano out, they chucked the box out without looking to see if there was anything else inside. Didn't they, mate?

MATE'S MATE

Yes, mate.

LORD

So, that's how you came to be in the box.

MATE & MATE'S MATE

No, no…

LORD

Never mind. Here comes Tom looking for some plot development, with Bessie, his pig.

(SFX – PIG)

TOM DUNG

Oh, what a lovely day for a walk in the Himalayas, eh, Bessie?

LORD

My name is Lord Double-Glazing. I'm the richest man in England. Look!

(SFX – UNDOING OF ZIP. MONEY SPILLING)

MATE

What a place to keep it.

LORD

How would you like to change places with me for fifteen seconds?

TOM DUNG

Hear that, Bessie? (SFX: RASPBERRY) There's a lot we can do in fifteen seconds. We could…

LORD

Yes, come along, come along. I grow tired of my wealth. Let's make the exchange now!

TOM DUNG

Oh so this is what it's like! First, Bessie, I'm going to buy a velvet coat for you, my favourite pig. Then I'll give a ball, a grand ball, and I must write the invitations quickly. And I'll get married to a princess, yes, there's still time. We'll have four children, and we'll be so happy. Now, what shall I call them? I'll call the first one Olive, I'll call the second Olive, and I'll call the third one Olive—oh wait, no I don't like that name… I'll call the fourth one Olive, and I'll call the second one Byron, and I'll call the fifth one Bicycle, and then, where's the Princess…

LORD

Fifteen!

TOM DUNG

Oh well Bessie, it was nice while it lasted. At least we can say we've been rich. And afterall, though fame and fortune has slipped away, I've still got the social disease. Got something to show for it.

LORD

You silly, twisted boy!

(GRAMS)

MILLIGAN / GERMAN DOCTOR

Zo, you think we're all in a BBC programme?

ANNOUNCER

Yes, doctor.

MILLIGAN / GERMAN DOCTOR

Very interesting. You're not in a hospital?

ANNOUNCER

Not really, no.

MILLIGAN / GERMAN DOCTOR

But you vant me to discharge you?

ANNOUNCER

That's true. Yes, doctor, because I have to announce the end of the show.

MILLIGAN / GERMAN DOCTOR

You're not happy here? Don't you like ze curtains?

ANNOUNCER

I love the curtains.

MILLIGAN / GERMAN DOCTOR

Well, I hate ze curtains! That drab green with the sickly yellow spots! Who can get avay with such curtains? Well, not me, baby! Get out of here! How dare you come into my office and play viz my curtains? I'll have to see my next patient. Terence Wacky?

ANNOUNCER

Look, please ask him doctor, how he intends to resolve the story that he swapped two babies at birth, the rich for the poor, and vice versa, to prove a revolutionary point?

WACKY

Hahah! You want to know how the story ends?

ANNOUNCER

Yes, please! For everyone's sake!

WACKY

(Manic laughing)

MILLIGAN / GERMAN DOCTOR

I'm afraid ve von't get any sense out of that chicken.

ANNOUNCER

Very well, but before I go doctor, I would like to say one final thing...

MILLIGAN / GERMAN DOCTOR

What's that?

ANNOUNCER

Take it away, boys!

(GRAMS IN STRONG)

The Great Escape! And I'm not even Steve McQueen—yet. Thank God—or whoever is wherever—that Spike was too depressed to insist the script be hacked around—OK sometimes for the better but how can you tell unless you play it? Anyway there was no undercurrent that The Milligan would not go onstage unless his demands were met and to be fair if he was trying it on we could have called him on it so it's no good always blaming Spike who by the way was brilliant tonight. He acted the script tonight, it was not necessary to send it up along the way—the writing supported us all!

Spike sensed the Old Man / Butler part and played it with a wonderful pathos—because he has genius in him—and tonight he did not try to improve his own performance. The audience loved him into it—magic!

Why am I going on? Well, I would, wouldn't I?

A lovely night out of nowhere and Spike went home without complaint. Who could live with that man?

PS Spike can be gentle, kind and considerate as if his suffering brings out these unlooked for qualities. Can I ever KNOW him? Perhaps only by knowing myself...

Hey, it's all a laugh, isn't it? Let's get laid, man! It's doing my head in! I'm famous if I go to the right places. There's a cellar under Leicester Square that serves hope after hours. But I'm trying to give it up...

Shut up, he explained.

EPISODE 4
THAT CAKE-ELUSIVE PIMPERNEL

Spike came in, not early, in good humour though—laughing and joking with John Bluthel about Australia and the town where his mother lived as being an above ground cemetery so he won't have to bury her when the time comes!

So I'll save on the cost of a burial plot and buy a sheep farm...

Won't that be expensive, asked Bluthal.

Not for one sheep, answered Spike.

One sheep could be lonely, Spike.

Nonsense, we'll have each other. We'd have a lot in common. We're both vegetarians.

A sheep is a ruminant, explained Chris Langham..

And I'm a room to let, said Spike.

Plenty of laughs and badinage at the read through today, like we were normal people doing a normal job like maybe digging a hole in the road because then somebody else could fill it in ... all good clean fun actually. Scary though! It could be all downhill from here...

Oh come on, chin up! This is how it's supposed to be... Fun, remember? Relax, are you some kind of control freak?

ANNOUNCER
The BBC present the Milligan papers by John Antrobus

(GRAMS IN STRONG)

ANNOUNCER
They seek him here, they seek him there, those Frenchies seek him everywhere. Is he in heaven, is he in hell? That cake elusive Pimpernel. The discerning amongst you may have noticed that I substituted the word "cake" instead of "damned". Well, we don't want that "damned" elusive Pimpernel on the BBC. "Cake" is a much nicer word—"that cake elusive Pimpernel." However, immediately following the substitution of the word "cake" into the latest script of The Milligan Papers, a meeting of the BBC board of governors was called.

OMNES
(Snoring, wheezing, ad-lib talking in sleep)

MILLIGAN / CHAIRMAN
Ladies and gentlemen, as chairman of the board of the Beeb, it is my unpleasant task...

BOARD MEMBER 1
Speaker! Speak for England!

BOARD MEMBER 2
Resign!

MILLIGAN / CHAIRMAN
Why should I? It's still got hairs on it!

BOARD MEMBER 2
Resign, it will please someone…

MILLIGAN / CHAIRMAN
I must draw your attention to the deliberate use of the word "cake" in the current Milligan Papers.

OMNES

Shame! Shame! Aye! This'll mean an election! Wash your mouth out! Etc.

MILLIGAN / CHAIRMAN

Now listen, it's not the word "cake" so much as the way that perverted announcer said it.

BOARD MEMBER 1

Flog him!

MILLIGAN / CHAIRMAN

What am I bid? (Got a reasonable laugh on that, continues with the show…) I think besting him will only encourage him. He went to a public school.

BOARD MEMBER 2

Couldn't we use the word "sandwich"?

MILLIGAN / CHAIRMAN

Sandwich?

BOARD MEMBER 2

Yes. Is he in heaven, or is he in hell? That sandwich-elusive Pimpernel.

BOARD MEMBER 1

Nonsense! The writer cannot be expected to make his bread and butter from 'sandwich.' Besides, what would be in the sandwich?

MILLIGAN / CHAIRMAN

Terry Wogan. He's in everything.

BOARD MEMBER 1

Bring back hanging or Eamonn Andrews.

BOARD MEMBER 2

We _are_ in danger!

BOARD MEMBER 1

Set fire to Broadcasting House!

GRAMS—DRAMATIC

POPPINGHAM

My name is Lord Poppingham. Pronounced (SFX—POP)-ingham. Known only to myself while taking a bath, as the Scarlet Pimpernel. This is because of a rash I developed while holidaying in Tangiers, where the camels are jolly friendly. (calls) Scrackle! Scrackle! Where is my faithful manservant?

MILLIGAN

In your underwear, like everybody else is.

POPPINGHAM (calling)

My valet! Scrackle! Scrackle!

MILLIGAN

You called, sir?

POPPINGHAM

I'm going out. Knock a hole in the wall.

MILLIGAN / SCRACKLE

Wouldn't you prefer to use the front door, sir?

POPPINGHAM

I can't be bothered with all that door nonsense. I'd have to go to all the trouble of walking down the hall.

MILLIGAN / SCRACKLE
It's a lot of work, knocking a hole through a wall, sir.

POPPINGHAM
What are you talking about?

MILLIGAN / SCRACKLE
About 30 words a minute, sir, which is the going rate for this type of show.

POPPINGHAM
Are the geese outside ready? I'm going to a policeman's ball.

MILLIGAN / SCRACKLE
How singular of you, sir

(SFX—GAS LEAKS)

POPPINGHAM
I ordered geese not gas leaks… Oh very well. Gee up, gooses!

(SFX—GEESE HONKING. CANTERING AWAY.)

ANNOUNCER
As the biggest fop in London aristocratic Society galloped through the streets with his geese, he stopped only to address a tree.

POPPINGHAM
Come on, stand up, you can do better than that!

ANNOUNCER
Meanwhile, across the channel, the French aristocracy were having a rotten time at the mercy of Madame Guillotine.

MILLIGAN
Off with their heads!

That Cake-Elusive Pimpernel

BBC RADIO MANAGER

Did someone say the word 'cake'? You know it is banned at the BBC...

OMNES
Off with their heads!

(SFX—DRUM ROLL. GUILLOTINE DROP. SLICE. PLOP.)

MAN
One hundred and eighty!

OMNES
(Cheering)

ROBESPIERRE
Ferme la porte!

(SFX – DOOR CLOSE.)

MILLIGAN
Monsieur Robespierre, the mob grow restless with their 'off with their heads'. The novelty is wearing off. We must think of something else.

ROBESPIERRE
How about 'off with their wedding tackle?'

MILLIGAN
We'd never get their wedding tackles passed the BBC.

ROBESPIERRE
I had no idea they were so big… I have invested heavily in all those guillotines. We must keep using them, we simply must!

MILLIGAN
Now, now, Robespierre, you mustn't lose your head over this. Get a hold of yourself.

ROBESPIERRE
How do I do that?

MILLIGAN
Let go of me first. I say we put them in the other way around and chop off their bodies.

ROBESPIERRE

That would mean the expense of bigger baskets.

MILLIGAN

There isn't a bigger basket than you, mate.

ROBESPIERRE

Shut up!

ANNOUNCER

And so the aristocrats were dragged to the Guillotine and put in the other way round.

MILLIGAN

Off with their bodies!

OMNES

Off with their bodies!

(SFX—DRUM ROLL. GUILLOTINE DROP. SLICE. PLOP.)

MAN

One hundred and ninety!

OMNES
(Cheering)

WOMAN
Oh, it's so much more fun shouting "off with their bodies".

OMNES
(Agree)

ANNOUNCER
Meanwhile, in London, the British aristocrats flaunted themselves with up to eighteen balls per week.

MILLIGAN
That's a lot of balls.

ANNOUNCER
Shut up! Dear God, I hope this isn't getting too left wing.

MAN
No, but it's getting a few laughs though.

POPPINGHAM
You know, I've every admiration for our own Aristocracy. There's nothing I like more than standing in the rain outside Westminster Abbey. I once had the good fortune to be splashed when her majesty's coach went past. Do you know, I've never had that dress dry-cleaned…

(GRAMS—SWING BAND. BALL ATMOSPHERE.)

POPPINGHAM
Lady Diana, may I have the pleasure of this next dance?

LADY DIANA
Certainly, I'll watch you.

POPPINGHAM
I made a wonderful couple as I waltzed across the ballroom, then I realised that Lady Diana was wearing her famous false teeth.

(GRAMS—DRAMATIC CHORD)

POPPINGHAM
The Diana Teeth, envy of London's society. I had a false, false set of Diana teeth made and for my own purposes, to be revealed later, I planned a daring switch. Lady Diana! Look into this bucket!

(SFX—SLAP. POP. TEETH CHATTER. TIN BUCKET.)

LADY DIANA
Ow! Where are my priceless teeth?

POPPINGHAM
Lady Diana, I happened to be passing and I've retrieved them from the prunes and custard.

(GRAMS)

ANNOUNCER
Having made the switch, Lord Poppingham left the ball and made his way to Dover.

OMNES
Make chicken noises.

POPPINGHAM
Can't you get these chickens to go any faster?

DRIVER
Being chickens is hard enough work without going anywhere.

ANNOUNCER
In Dover, Lord Poppingham met secretly with a farm labourer, one, Big Dick Scratcher.

DICK
Oh God bless ye, young master. Did you bring the teeth, sire?

POPPINGHAM
Yes I did. They're the finest in the land. They should do the trick.

(SFX—TEETH CHATTER.)

DICK
Right. I'll start digging the channel escape tunnel immediately, sire. (GROANS)

SFX—TEETH CHATTER.

POPPINGHAM
Now, Big Dick, during that appalling impression of a man digging, it's time I told you my real identity. The question is, can you be trusted?

DICK
In a word, no.

POPPINGHAM
Are you telling the truth?

DICK
Yes.

POPPINGHAM
In that case, you can be trusted. I'd like you to refer to me as (DRAMATIC CHORDS) The Scarlet Pimpernel.

DICK
But if I don't know who you are, sir, how will I recognise you?

POPPINGHAM
I give up Big Dick. (No, wait, sorry, I give up, Big Dick.) How will you recognise me? Well don't worry, we'll think of something.

DICK
I've thought of something.

POPPINGHAM
What?

DICK
Arabia.

POPPINGHAM
...No, that doesn't really help... Now, no one must know about this tunnel, not even anyone. Otherwise they'll all want one.

ANNOUNCER
Through constant overtime digging, Lady Diana's teeth broke down. Lord Poppingham took to the dark streets of London, determined to replace them.

OMNES
(Chickens).

That Cake-Elusive Pimpernel

POPPINGHAM
Stop! Stop here, driver! Woah! Woah!

(SFX—FOOTSTEPS....SLAP. POP. TEETH CHATTER. TIN BUCKET.)

MILLIGAN
Stop! Stop thief! My teeth!

(SFX—GROANING/LABOURING, DIGGING, TEETH CHATTERING)

ANNOUNCER
The sound you hear is that of the channel tunnel being dug with teeth, when in fact it's a BBC employee behind me rattling two pebbles in a box. Meanwhile Lord Poppingham continued his preparations to steal away the French aristocracy from the terrors of the guillotine.

"We are looking for a new head of Government..."

(SFX—DOOR KNOCKING)

MILLIGAN
Hold on a minute. I'm just emptying the po out of the window.

(SFX—SLOPPING.)

POPPINGHAM
Ugh!

MILLIGAN
Oh, sorry sir.

(SFX—DOOR OPENING)

POPPINGHAM
Scrackle?

MILLIGAN
Sir?

POPPINGHAM
The towel.

MILLIGAN
Towel coming, sir.

POPPINGHAM
Now, knock a hole in that wall.

(SFX—WALL COLLAPSING)

POPPINGHAM
Thank you.

MILLIGAN
Sir, would you say you were an eccentric?

POPPINGHAM

Nonsense. I'm church of England.

(SFX – RASPBERRY)

MILLIGAN

Would you like anything else, sir?

POPPINGHAM

Yes, would you please put that po back under the bed.

MILLIGAN

I can't sir. You see, the steam rusts the springs.

POPPINGHAM

Yes. Now, look here.

MILLIGAN

Where?

POPPINGHAM

Here! I believe you're a whistling expert. Now, between you and I and this mustn't go further than you,

MILLIGAN

What's that rash on your boat-race-face?

POPPINGHAM

It's a souvenir from Tangiers. Mr. Scrackle, I have a secret mission to save the French aristocracy from nicotine.

MILLIGAN

You mean guillotine?

POPPINGHAM

No, this one just gives them a nasty nic. (LAUGHS) Oh dear.

MILLIGAN

Off with their bodies!

OMNES

Off with their bodies!

(SFX—DRUM ROLL. GUILLOTINE DROP. SLICE. PLOP.)

MAN

Three hundred and twenty!

POPPINGHAM

I can't bear to hear those awful sounds of the mob! Can't you put some French revolution crowd excluder around the door?

MILLIGAN

The badly acted sounds of the French mob are coming through the holes in the wall, sir.

POPPINGHAM

Well yes, in that case we had better lower our trousers and think of England. Now, as the Scarlet Pimpernel, I need a secret whistle. But of course I daren't do it myself, it would give me away.

MILLIGAN

You could try whistling inside a sock, sir.

POPPINGHAM

No, I'm afraid I don't know that one.

MILLIGAN

Listen monsieur, I could do the secret whistling for you.

POPPINGHAM
That would be marvellous, Scrackle. But first I'd like to hear some samples of your whistling.

MILLIGAN (Dee-dees to the tune of 'Lambeth Walk')

POPPINGHAM
What's that?

MILLIGAN
What's that? That's me whistling.

POPPINGHAM
It sounds like singing.

MILLIGAN
Ah, that's because it's disguised!

POPPINGHAM
But it doesn't sound the way that the Scarlet Pimpernel would whistle.

MILLIGAN
I'll try something else.

SFX KAZOO

POPPINGHAM
That's it! By Jove, he's got it!

MILLIGAN
Yes, and wait till I see her!

POPPINGHAM
Come with me, the Scarlet Pimpernel! Accompany me to France and whistle, strike terror into the hearts of the commune with added VAT—and bring hope to the flower of the French Aristocracy!

(GRAMS)

ANNOUNCER
Back in England, the secret escape tunnel was coming along famously. The farm-labouring oaf, Big Dick Scratcher, was getting rid of the dirt by selling it to The Sun. Alas, the false teeth that were admirably employed kept wearing out. Unlike George Chisholm and his gentlemen of jazz!

GEORGE CHISHOLM AND HIS GENTLEMEN OF JAZZ

(SFX—FOOTSTEPS….SLAP. POP. TEETH CHATTER. TIN BUCKET.)

MILLIGAN
My teeth! My teeth!

ANNOUNCER
As George Chisholm and his thugs vandalised the mouths of Londoners, Lord Poppiingham met with Lady Diana for a meal.

(SFX: SWING BAND. CUTLERY / CROCKERY ETC.)

LADY DIANA
That's very nice crockery Lord, but where's the dinner?

POPPINGHAM
Oh, there is no dinner, this is a 'sound-of-cutlery-and-crockery' restaurant.

LADY DIANA
Listen, Lord (POP)ingham… Do you know the identity of the Scarlet Pimpernel?

POPPINGHAM
No why?

LADY DIANA
Because my niece, the beautiful, diseased Louise Antoinette, is in the hands and knees and…

OMNES
Boompsidaisi!

LADY DIANA
Of Le Robespierre.

ANNOUNCER
Oh, how Lord Poppingham longed to cry out—

POPPINGHAM
I am the Scarlet Pimpernel! And I like wearing women's clothing!

LADY DIANA
Listen to me. Louise Antoinette faces the guillotine in a month's time.

POPPINGHAM
What? With her connections, she shouldn't have to wait that long. I can arrange to have her done privately. (laughs)

ANNOUNCER
Laughing outside, crying inside, for Lord Poppingham loved Louise Antoinette. She must never know of his plans to rescue her. "What kind of fool am I? That never fell in love…"

(SFX—SLAP. POP. TEETH CHATTER. TIN BUCKET.)

ANNOUNCER (minus teeth)
My false teeth! This time, they've gone too far. They'll pay for this.

MILLIGAN
So saying, he held up a small bag of crisps. Meanwhile, back at the French Revolution, Monsieur Robespierre had an unexpected visitor.

(SFX—DOOR OPEN)

MILLIGAN / SCRACKLE
Ah! Monsieur Robespierre,

(SFX—TOILET CHAIN)

MILLIGAN / SCRACKLE
I'm terribly sorry, madam.

(SFX—DOOR CLOSE. DOOR OPEN)

ROBESPIERRE
In here, you fool!

MILLIGAN / SCRACKLE
Ah! Monsieur Robespierre!

ROBESPIERRE
Did anyone see you come in?

MILLIGAN / SCRACKLE
Only France.

ROBESPIERRE
Then we are discovered.

MILLIGAN / SCRACKLE
Listen Robespierre, le mob are now tired of saying 'off with their bodies'.

ROBESPIERRE
Ok, then how about 'off with their knickers'?

MILLIGAN / SCRACKLE
Do you think that will terrify the French Aristocracy?

ROBESPIERRE
In cold weather, yes.

MILLIGAN / SCRACKLE
So, how about 'off with their knickers' and then let the cold tap run over their bum?

ROBESPIERRE
C'est brilliante!

MILLIGAN / SCRACKLE
Off with their knickers and let the cold tap run over their bum!

OMNES
Off with their knickers and let the cold tap run over their bum!

(SFX—DRUM ROLL. GUILLOTINE DROP. SLICE. PLOP.)

MAN
Five hundred and seventy!

OMNES
(Cheering)

GRAMS

(SFX—KAZOO)

ANNOUNCER
The Scarlet Pimpernel had decided to book Herbert Scrackle and his whistles into Les Folies Bergère. Unfortunately, the first night of Mr Scrackle's amazing performance of bird impressions coincided with the first performance of Le Petomane. Likewise, the open season for shooting. We all know how le French love song birds.

(SFX—WHISTLING. GUN FIRE. SCREAMS.)

MILLIGAN
You bleedin' thugs!

OMNES
(Protests, ad-lib)

ANNOUNCER
In the interests of decorum, would you substitute with the word "cake"?

MILLIGAN
Right… You bleedin' cake!

ANNOUNCER
On this, I was immediately summoned before the board of governors.

OMNES
(Sleeping / ad-libbing)

BOARD MEMBER 1
Gentlemen, I see no reason why we shouldn't carry advertising on the tale of our shirts? Particularly outside of the curry season.

BOARD MEMBER 2
What about stains?

MILLIGAN / CHAIRMAN
Never mind Staines, what about Catford?

BOARD MEMBER 1
There are too many rude nature programmes.

OMNES
Yes / yes

BOARD MEMBER 2
Yes indeed. All these nudie gorillas. It really is quite shocking.

MILLIGAN / CHAIRMAN
They should have their hairies covered with trousers.

BOARD MEMBER 1
I know a good Jewish tailor.

GRAMS

ANNOUNCER
I couldn't get the board of governors to review my case that time. Meanwhile, back at the French Revolution, the naughty Robespierre was having it away with Louise Antoi—I beg your pardon—was having his way with Louise Antoinette.

ROBESPIERRE
I insist ma cherie. Je suis fatigue.

LOUISE
No Monsieur, not over here.

ROBESPIERRE
Oui, I am holding all the cards.

LOUISE
Oh, not another game of three-card-brag.

(SFX—KAZOO)

ROBESPIERRE
There is something in the wardrobe…

(SFX—DOOR OPEN)

ANNOUNCER
With Herbert Scrackle the whistler stood a tall masked stranger, who had not adjusted his dress before leaving.

ROBESPIERRE
And who are you, tall masked stranger?

POPPINGHAM
I can never reveal my true identity.

ROBESPIERRE
Why not? You're revealing everything else.

POPPINGHAM
But I must never reveal my real self to Louise Antoinette.

LOUISE
Well I don't care, as long as you pay cash, dear.

POPPINGHAM
I have come to take you home to England. Homeward my beauty.

LOUISE
I'm doing much better here cherie, thank you. Now what do you want? The black stockings? Or the nuns gear with the jelly massage?

POPPINGHAM
Louise, I know you take me to be an utter prat. But what would you say if I told you that I was the Scarlet Pimpernel?

LOUISE
I'd say you were an even bigger prat. I mean, look at you! You're covered in oil!

MILLIGAN / OLD BUTLER
He's an Noilly Prat!

POPPINGHAM
Shut up! In that case I'll have the jelly in black stockings and the nuns massage at close range, thank you.

ANNOUNCER
Yes, you've been listening to England's only show without Terry Wogan. And now, my final number. 'What kind of fool am I?'

MILLIGAN
We give up.

ANNOUNCER
'That never fell in love…'

(SFX—DRUM ROLL. GUILLOTINE DROP. SLICE. PLOP.)

MAN
One thousand and ninety!

OMNES
Hooray!

THE END.

All I can say is, we got away with it! The writing so thin! It was the cast and of course Spike who made the evening work—with the help of a sympathetic audience come to visit and cheer up a sick patient! OK, confession over. Thank whoever, wherever, that Spike was not on a downer tonight. With his help the Titanic did not sink and the ice was confined to tinkling of glasses, scotch and soda! Nobody even mentioned the paucity of the script (OK, enough of that, right? You have the right to be less than perfect, darling. Everyone gets by from time to time).

And so into the sweet night, relieved!

EPISODE 5
THE INCURABLES (PART 1)

By John Antrobus

Spike has turned up today with a contempt for humanity which he describes as a failed evolutionary experiment. As failed evolutionary experiments we continue with the read through which of course is pointless in terms of being a doomed species. As part of Spikes disgust today will be his contempt for the audience—not uncommon—' Anything to make the idiots laugh!' which excuses any corny additions to the script... ' They won't know the difference', he says. I try and keep my script intelligent and refreshing but... what? The whole series concept I sold to the BBC on the name of Spike Milligan, so now there is a price to pay—NO MILLIGAN—NO SHOW!!

Whatever happened to Love, Light and Peace, Spike? Isn't that how you sign your letters and autographs?

Monster Milligan is on the rampage! Prayer is the only answer...

PRESENTER
The BBC proudly present "The Milligan Papers" written by John Antrobus. The Incurables—Part One! Beware, listeners—this episode is contagious!

MILLIGAN / McGONAGALL
Oh! Great Britain was set in the silver BBC
World War II had started and oh, dearie, dearie me
For the Germans had just overrun most of France
And were leading the Allies a terrible dance
Like the tango.
Ohh, the British expeditionary force ran like the clappers for Dunkirk
And soon the whole British army were out of work
Most got away, by the skin of their teeth
Others got away with little boats with the sea beneath
Instead of on top, which would have been quite a lot...

ANNOUNCER
Beleaguered Britain in 1941, later to be known as 1942. Little England faced the Nazis across the channel. But it did little good, they were too far away to be seen. Meanwhile, in a bunker below Whitehall, the prim monster Winston Churchill and his chief of staff, Field Marshall Alan Brookes, worked to bring victory to the Allies, a defeat to the Axis and a draw for the Australians.

(SFX: DRAMATIC MUSIC)

CHURCHILL
Right, Brookie. Read back that memo.

BROOKES / MILLIGAN
Urgent that you defend Singapore, stroke Malta, stroke India, stroke Benghazi, stroke the cat... to the last man, and then let me have his name.

The Incurables (Part 1)

CHURCHILL

Now, how many of our overseas positions are left?

BROOKES / MILLIGAN

Oh, they're all left sir. But mostly, in enemy hands.

CHURCHILL

Brilliant tactics, Brookie. They will have the illusion that they are winning the war.

BROOKES / MILLIGAN

While we have the illusion that we are losing it, sir.

CHURCHILL

Right, send a telegram to the First Lord of the Admiralty. Tell him to sink the German ships, sink the Bismark, sink the Nürnberg, sink the Tirpitz.

BROOKES / MILLIGAN

Any more, sir?

CHURCHILL

Yes, sink The Prince Of Wales before they do... That's enough sinking for now, Brookie. Now, what's the time?

BROOKES / MILLIGAN

I'mx sorry sir, that's restricted information. Remember sir, walls have ears.

CHURCHILL

They also have sausages... You know, I'm getting fed up with this war, Brookie. It's holding up my memoirs. We must stop sending reinforcements to Singapore.

BROOKES / MILLIGAN
Why?

CHURCHILL
Because if they hold out against the Japs, it means I'll have to re-write two whole chapters.

BROOKES / MILLIGAN
But we are trying to keep up with your war memoirs, sir. We were only one day out with Dunkirk.

CHURCHILL
Ah. We will fight them on the beaches. We will fight them in the fields. We will fight them in the cities. We will never surrender.

BROOKES / MILLIGAN
Oh, very funny sir.

CHURCHILL
Now, how are these secret weapons coming along?

(BROOKES performs DRAMATIC CHORD)

BROOKES / MILLIGAN
Which one was that sir?

CHURCHILL
Well, of course, the dried prune bomb. A brilliant idea of the beavers to get together the last unused stocks of dried prunes into a ginormous prune bomb. Imagine all that dysentery, all that.... er... all that—

BROOKES / MILLIGAN
Doom, sir?

CHURCHILL

-doom, in one prune… er… one prune…—

BROOKES / MILLIGAN

Bomb, sir?

CHURCHILL

-bomb… Exploding over the Third Reich with an almighty… an almighty…

BROOKES / MILLIGAN

(RASPBERRY), sir?

CHURCHILL

(RASPBERRY) Exactly yes.

BROOKES / MILLIGAN

Towel, nurse… There's been an accident!

CHURCHILL

I'll open a window.

BROOKES / MILLIGAN

Too late! It's here. I'm sorry to say sir, that the dried prune experiment has gone badly wrong. Someone in the laboratory dropped a test tube and then the whole team contracted an incurable disease, code name Green Swan.

CHURCHILL

Has anyone died of it yet?

The Incurables (Part 1)

BROOKES / MILLIGAN

Forty people died. Apart from that, nobody died at all.

CHURCHILL

I say, Brookie. Was Vera Lynn among the casualties?

BROOKES / MILLIGAN

No, sir.

CHURCHILL

Anne Shelton?

BROOKES / MILLIGAN

No.

CHURCHILL

Charlie Chester?

BROOKES / MILLIGAN

No, sir.

CHURCHILL

Haven't you got any good news for me?

BROOKES / MILLIGAN

Yes, sir. Tommy Handley's got piles.

CHURCHILL

Piles of what?

BROOKES / MILLIGAN

(RASPBERRY)

CHURCHILL

Oh Thank God. I tell you what, Brookie, I've had a brilliant idea. We'll reform the survivors into a suicide squad called 'The Royal Household Incurables'.

BROOKES / MILLIGAN

(Dramatic chords: Pom-pom-pom-pom) Sir?

CHURCHILL

Yes. We can drop these highly contagious men behind enemy lines where they will copulate in a military manner.

BROOKES / MILLIGAN

One-two-three, one-two-three?

CHURCHILL

Exactly. Passing on the disease until it reaches (sung) pom-pom-pom-pom-pom (spoken) Hitler.

BROOKES / MILLIGAN

Gad!

CHURCHILL

In these hard times, Brookie, we must make our own dramatic chords.

(BROOKES and CHURCHILL continue with the dramatic chords)

ANNOUNCER
Meanwhile, in huts on the Duke of Hamilton's estate in Skipland, where the victims of the dried prune experiment were into free-fall conversation:

(DRAMATIC CHORD)

HARRY
Yes, for those without televisions, here we are on the Duke of Hamilton's estate in Skipland, SW14.

TOM
Yes, and I must say I feel decidedly better.

HARRY
Better than what, Tom?

TOM
Better than very, very ill. Yes, today I just feel very ill.

JOHN
Shut up! Can't you see we're all (sung) doom-doom-doom-doomed?

MILLIGAN
One more time!

JOHN

Doom-doom-doom-doomed.

TOM

Good God, he's caught Beethoven's Fifth!

HARRY

John is trying to say that we are (sung) doom-doom-doom-doomed, Tom.

JOHN

I know what I'm trying to say, Harry. It's no thanks to you that we're all in this predicament! It was you who dropped the test tube and gave us all the (sung) doom-doom-doom-doom's. Swine! I'll throttle you.

HARRY

No, calm down John. Overacting will never get you anywhere except the National. We must all realise that code name Green Swan, this illness, causes severe hormonal sex changes and keep your hands to yourself.

JOHN

I know, darling. I've been thinking about this, dearest.

TOM

Well done, but thinking about this dearest is not something you working class should attempt without protective clothing.

(GRAMS)

The Incurables (Part 1)

ANNOUNCER
Unbeknownst to the bickering Incurables, events were now taking a drastic dong. From a lone German plane, a lone parachute descended. It was a lone Rudolph Hess carrying a lone Third Reich plastic bag. But in 1941, plastic bags were still in the experimental stage and liable to explode if—

(SFX: EXPLOSION FOLLOWED BY SCREAM)

HESS / MILLIGAN
Ach, Himmel! Thank goodness, I landed on something soft. Thank you, Raquel Welsh. Now. Ah! A note! What does this note say? 'Do not enter. Contagious disease. Incurable material and doom-doom-doom-doom'? Good job I can't read. Please, mein effects.

(SFX: DOOR OPENING)

HESS / MILLIGAN
Thank you—oh, my finger! Good evening! Subtitle: guten abend.

OMNES
Good evening.

(SFX: DOOR OPENING)

NURSE
Oh, we weren't expecting any new patients. Have you caught it?

HESS / MILLIGAN
No, but if you could spare the time I can provide the body! Ha! Made in Germany! Seif Heil! I never said that...

NURSE
Let's have a few details, shall we?

HESS
Only my k-name, k-rank, and k-number.

NURSE
K-name?

HESS
K-name is K-Rudolph K-Hess.

NURSE
K-rank?

HESS
K-Deputy.

NURSE
K-number?

HESS
K-number two, if you'll pardon the expression.

NURSE
Right. You'll find some clean pyjamas on that patient over there.

HESS
We do not wear pyjamas in the Third Reich. We only wear (sung) bum-bum-bum-bum. Wagner's Flight of the Valkyries!

(FLIGHT OF THE VALKYRIES PLAYS; HESS OVER TOP SHOUTS 'GO WAGNER GO! LISTEN TO THOSE FRENCH HORNS GO! GO DADDY DADDY!' etc)

JOHN
Why hasn't Nurse Carruthers caught code name Green Swan? She comes and goes in this ward with impunity. Why? How? When? Which? Who? etcetera.

The Incurables (Part 1)

TOM
Nurse Carruthers has a very very rare blood group, Rhesus Spok Negative. Only previously known in the Tuwaki Wallaby, now extinct.

JOHN
Why?

TOM
Well, we think it's because Nurse Carruthers drained all its blood. You see, the white corpuscle outnumbered the red by a huge amount in Rhesus Spok Negative.

HARRY
Could you amplify that?

TOM
Yes. (THROUGH A MEGAPHONE) The red corpuscle are—

NARRATOR
If I might come in here.

TOM (MEGAPHONE)
Yes, come in here if you like, but remember we have the negatives of you interviewing sheep at the Dorchester Hotel!

NARRATOR
It's quite obvious, listeners, that no one has any idea how Nurse Carruthers can come and go in the ward with impunity and not catch the Green Swan. But we at the BBC do not believe that our listeners should be able to pick holes in our entertainment programming. And so now, over to the inside of Nurse Carruthers' bloodstream, for an exclusive interview with a white corpuscle.

WHITE CORPUSCLE
(crackly) Testing, testing... yes, alright.

NEWS PRESENTER (mid-European/Dracula voice)
Yes, we proudly present Down Your Blood.

(SFX: SWEEPING ORCHESTRAL MUSIC)

NEWS PRESENTER
Good afternoon, and welcome to Down Your Blood. And here we are in a very pleasant spot in a main vein, near Nurse Carruthers' artery. And standing beside me is a White Corpuscle. Hello, White Corpuscle.

WHITE CORPUSCLE (AUSTRALIAN)
G'day, cobber.

NEWS PRESENTER
Good day.

WHITE CORPUSCLE
And four eggs up your wombat.

NEWS PRESENTER
That's very kind of you. How are you finding the blood flow here in this particular artery?

WHITE CORPUSCLE
Oh it come and goes, you know... We lost a couple of lads in the local action last night though.

NEWS PRESENTER
Oh, how upsetting. How did you lose them?

WHITE CORPUSCLE

Well, the nurse cut herself while shaving her legs and they fell out.

NEWS PRESENTER

In that case, she must be a short Irishman.

WHITE CORPUSCLE

What do you mean, a short Irishman?

NEWS PRESENTER

Anaemic.

WHITE CORPUSCLE

You Pommie bastard, come here! Bloody come here—(overlap presenter arguing)

ANNOUNCER

So, while they sort that out, let's hear some peace music from George Chisholm and his Gentlemen of Jazz.

(GEORGE CHISHOLM INTERLUDE)

ANNOUNCER

Over now to Idi Amin Crescent, Golders Green, to join two typical Radio 4 listeners or four typical Radio 2 listeners.

(SFX: IRON)

LISTENER 1 / MILLIGAN

What are you doing, darling?

LISTENER 2

I'm listening to the steam iron.

LISTENER 1 / MILLIGAN

Steam iron? What have you got it on, darling?

LISTENER 2
I've got it on synthetics. It's a great programme for nylon knickers.

LISTENER 1 / MILLIGAN
Oh, oh.

(SFX: KNOCKING)

LISTENER 2
Oh, there's someone at the door. You're not going to look, are you?

LISTENER 1 / MILLIGAN
No. That would spoil the surprise.

(SFX: KNOCKING, THEN DOORBELL)

LISTENER 1 / MILLIGAN
Oh, kinky.

LISTENER 2
You better answer it; it could be my brother Charlie.

(SFX: KNOCKING)

LISTENER 1 / MILLIGAN
It doesn't sound like your Charlie's knocking. It could be Eamonn Andrews and Ester Rantzen in 'This Is Your Dad's Life'. I'll just have a peep. (PEEP) That's better. Now I'll see who it is.

(SFX: DOOR OPENS)

BBC REPRESENTATIVE
Hello. I am from the BBC. We are researching to see how many people am still listening to ITMA.

LISTENER 1 / MILLIGAN
Was that you knocking?

The Incurables (Part 1)

BBC REPRESENTATIVE
Oh yes.

LISTENER 1
Well don't stop. We're just getting used to it.

(SFX: DOOR SLAMS)

ANNOUNCER
Here we put a stop to this tiresome conversation—

LISTENER 1 / MILLIGAN
Oh, the show's over…

ANNOUNCER
Meanwhile, back at the hut, Tom confronts Rudolph Hess. (DRAMATIC CHORDS)

TOM
Wait just a moment. I don't remember you working with us in the laboratory?

HESS / MILLIGAN
You do not remember me working with you in the lavatory? You have a good mind, and you win the Flasher of the Year award—a waist high practice mirror.

TOM
I'll have to reflect on that for a moment.

HARRY
Now you've fallen in with us, chummie, you will have contracted Green Swan.

HESS / MILLIGAN
Thinks. What is this Green Swan?

HARRY

Green Swan is a highly contagious lethal disease.

HESS

(STARTS LAUGHING). What is this Green Swan?

TOM

It's a mix of whooping cough, water-bed measles, amoebic dysentery, rice blast, anthrax, the common cold, and two weeks in Scunthorpe.

HESS / MILLIGAN

Do you know that, apart from Russia, the Fuhrer has never had ein headache?

TOM

Well, we'll give him one, eh chaps? (sounds of agreement)

JOHN

No, count me out.

(SFX: HITTING NOISE)

JOHN

Ow!

HESS / MILLIGAN

One, two, three... coming up nine, ten, out!

JOHN

I'm not interested in the war.

HESS / MILLIGAN

Or in that joke, by the sound of it. You will form a government lying on the floor in exile, and accept an armistice!

(SFX: DRAMATIC MUSIC)

The Incurables (Part 1)

HESS / MILLIGAN

See, we Germans don't have to make our own dramatic chords.

ANNOUNCER

(sung in the style of a prayer) 'And so the peace armistice was signed between Germany and John Smith by the government of Great Britain in exile of Incurables'

(ALL SING 'AMEN')

ANNOUNCER

And that night, on the rooftop of the Daily Mirror building in Fleet Street, a lone fire-watcher waited for the onslaught of the Luftwaffe.

(FIRE-WATCHER SINGS)

FIRE-WATCHER / MILLIGAN

Now, where did I put me stirrup pump? Ah, here, inside me trousers. Oh, that's not it. I wish it was. Oh mate, I don't 'arf fancy a cigarette. I think I may strike a light.

(SFX: MATCH STRIKE)

FIRE-WATCHER / MILLIGAN

Gosh, strike a light! Now, where did I put me bucket of sand? It's over there with the duck.

(SFX: QUACKING)

FIRE-WATCHER / MILLIGAN

I don't see the point of this duck watching. Why does the Luftwaffe want to bomb a duck at any rate?

CHURCHILL

Because I'm in it!

FIRE-WATCHER / MILLIGAN
Ah, Mr Prime Minister. Listen.

(SFX: QUACKING)

FIRE-WATCHER / MILLIGAN
I don't think they're gonna come tonight. Arrrghhh! Me hand!

VOICE ON LOUDSPEAKER
Put that hand out!

FIRE-WATCHER / MILLIGAN
I could do with a hand out!

VOICE ON LOUDSPEAKER
Shut up!

(SFX: QUACKING)

ANNOUNCER
The match fell from the fire-watcher's scorched fingers onto a pile of old newspapers, causing this sound effect.

(SFX: FIRE CRACKLING, FIRE AMBULANCE BELL)

VOICES IN CHORUS
The conflagration spread down Fleet Street, up Robert Maxwell's trousers, until soon the whole city was ablaze. That was an actor's equity full employment announcement.

(SFX: QUACKING, FIRE, TRAFFIC)

ANNOUNCER
Meanwhile in Berlin, Goebbels broadcast to the world in a new propaganda offensive. Look out, Tommy!

(SFX: RADIO CRACKLING, TUNING ETC)

The Incurables (Part 1)

RADIO VOICE

Germany calling… Germany calling!

GOEBBELS

Hello American creeps. This is your friendly German raids calling America. Hello kids! We are simple, happy, jazz-loving krauts, trying to stop the decadent, sex-mad British from ruling the world! Hello, President Roosevelt! Hello Teddy! For your delight, we bring you the old Deutschland Hot Shots! On piano, Hermann Goering!

GOERING
Yeah, baby!

GOEBBELS
On drums yours truly, voted number one snazzy dresser and chicken-sexer, Joseph "Sticks" Goebbels!

(JAZZ MUSIC PLAYS)

GOEBBELS
And now, putting it all together in modern style, our leader and number one, Adolf "Its the Gypsy in Me" Hitler!

HITLER/MILLIGAN
(Sings)
Is you is or is you int mein baby?

OMNES
Heil!

HITLER/MILLIGAN
Is you is or is you int mein baby now?

GOERING
Crazy, daddy!

GOEBBELS
I say, I say, I say!

HITLER / MILLIGAN
What do you say, you say, you say, daddy?

More of Spike as Hitler, in rehearsal!

GOEBBELS
What do you hope to get from the new scene, man?

HITLER/MILLIGAN
Well, Joe, all the goose stepping crap is finished! All the zeig-heiling is out, out! It's new scene, man! A smile, a song, and a concentration camp! Okay, boys, let's go! (German)
Sings...
Is you is or is you int mein baby?

OMNES

Heil!

HITLER/MILLIGAN

Is you is or is you int mein baby now?

OMNES

Heil!

HITLER/MILLIGAN

Don't forget, a nose job won't save you! Now for my Country and Leibestraum favourite ...

(Sings)

I was only twenty four hours from Moscow...!

Only twenty four hours from your arm....ament factories!

GOEBBELS

And there we are signing off now. Happy times! You folks in the USA, this is a broadcast from Germany downtown home of good jazz!

HITLER / MILLIGAN

Goodnight, Aryan folk. Sorry about ze Dunkirk. And remember: we will destroy you.

The Incurables (Part 1)

BOTH SING
I wonder who's whipping him now.
I wonder who's teaching him how
I wonder who's looking into her knees,
Ready for sleaze..
Eager to please... !!

ANNOUNCER

Fade out quickly ! Theme music! End credits please!

(END CREDITS)

The miracle happened! Love won out! Monster Milligan vanished into the haze and back up the mountain, don't go looking for it!

Love, Light and Pease returned. Spike even signed some autographs using those words...

Thank whoever, wherever...

Paul Spencer (producer) looks relieved. His job is secure for the moment and as there is only one more show to go he might survive this series—if he does not suffer a heart attack.

As to the other actors, well they're actors aren't they? It's employment! They're grateful for the gig! Best way to be...

But I want to be a successful evolutionary experiment, is this PRIDE?

Goodnight...

EPISODE 6
THE INCURABLES (PART 2)

Written by John Antrobus

Last day, six episode series! Before the read through Spike announced to one and all,

' Don't worry, there won't be a second series. The BBC hates me and I hate them. Small minds flatter you until they can get close enough to destroy you ' (that's worth a quote)

The Milligan seems quite happy to be despised by the Beeb and to enjoy a mutual loathing, all in his mind because the hierarchy at the BBC are tolerant of Spikes moods and bear his outbursts with good humour—after all most of them, ex-army officers, think ...

' In the National interest we survived Dunkirk, the battle for El Alamein and Arnhem so dealing with outbreaks of Milligan is no big deal. Though it may have cost us a few producer nervous breakdowns we must expect to take casualties,,,'

On with the show!

ANNOUNCER
The BBC proudly presents "The Milligan Papers", written by John Antrobus. The Incurables—Part Two. The gripping, nail-biting, toe sucking conclusion to our series...

(GRAMS IN STRONG)

McGONAGALL / MILLIGAN
Ohhhhh....
Here on the moors I am alone
With heather, gorse—nay microphone!
The sea winds up my kilt do blow..
Refreshing what's kept down below.
As brave Scots Guards charge, their kilts asunder
The hun can only look on in wonder!
And laying their machine guns well aside,
Take photos of it all! As would the blushing bride.
Ohhh, let us forget the dreadful times of war,
As do the copulating animals upon this windswept moor...

ANNOUNCER
Thank you, Mr McGonagall. You win a free burial at sea with a woman of your own choice. And now to the concluding part of our current serial.

MILLIGAN
I didn't know our cereal had currants in it!

(SFX: CLANG)

MILLIGAN
Ow!

The Incurables (Part 2)

The BBC Radio Announcer plays the BBC ANNOUNCER — but which one is he now? (In a locked ward with Terence Wacky)

ANNOUNCER

"Ow" exactly. Bang boom crash. World War II. Rocky III. After a disastrous experiment with a prune bomb (SFX: RASPBERRY) three British scientists contracted an incurable disease, code-name 'Green Swan', and were incarcerated in a hut at 'The Duke of Hamilton's Estate in Scotland, W1'. New readers start here.

(SFX: OMINOUS MUSIC, CRASHING, AIR RAID SIRENS)

ANNOUNCER
As bombs dropped on London, the prim monster was working deep in his bunker under Whitehall.

(SFX: POURING WATER. SLURPING)

CHURCHILL
Ah. Nothing like the sound effect of whisky being drunk to buck you up. I hope I said that right. Now, where's my list of good books to shorten the war? 'The Man That Never Was.' By Danny Le Rue.

CRUMBLING / MILLIGAN
Ah, oh. Good morning, sir. I've got that written down on my cuff.

CHURCHILL
What do you say in the afternoon?

CRUMBLING / MILLIGAN
I have to change my shirt, sir. I don't know yet. Your physician, Lord Moron and his enema, are outside sir.

CHURCHILL
Tell him I'm too ill to see him, friend or enema. Now, stop playing my butler, and change your voice to play Field Marshall Allan Brooke.

CRUMBLING / MILLIGAN
Certainly sir. I'll just put this rat-trap in my y-fronts.

CHURCHILL
Y-fronts?

CRUMBLING / MILLIGAN
Why not?

(SFX: RAT TRAP SNAP)

FIELD MARSHALL / MILLIGAN
Ahh-oooh. (much higher voice) You wanted to see my new voice, sir?

CHURCHILL
Ah, I see you've got them in a rat trap.

FIELD MARSHALL / MILLIGAN
(pained) Yes, sir.

CHURCHILL
What is Lord Moron hanging round outside for?

FIELD MARSHALL / MILLIGAN
Ah! It's about your book, sir. You, of course, are first in the writing of your war memoirs in advance of the events—which we are busy manipulating for you.

CHURCHILL
We need several major defeats to make it look as if we are losing the war—and then inspired by my magical leadership the climate begins to change...

BROOKE / MILLIGAN
Quite, quite, sir... But Lord Moron wants you to be down in chapter 7 of <u>his</u> memoirs with an attack of dysentery in Marrakech, in 1943.

CHURCHILL
That's impossible. I will not have dysentery to oblige every Tom, Dick and Harry. Circulate that as a memo!

FIELD MARSHALL / MILLIGAN

There's a telegram from Comrade Stalin and his moustache sir. It says: 'Please launch second front immediately.'

CHURCHILL

Ah, that red twit. (spits) Ah, there goes the phone. We have to cue our effects.

(SFX: PHONE RINGING. CHURCHILL ANSWERS)

CHURCHILL

Hello? The Prim Monster here.

STALIN

(Russian accent) Hello, Winston. (spits) Stalin here. How are you?

CHURCHILL

I'm very well, Jo. (spits)

STALIN

You must launch the second front immediately.

CHURCHILL

Never in the history of the world have so many owed so much to so few.

STALIN

Winston! (spits) In your next convoy, send us Vera Lynn and George Formby.

CHURCHILL

Why?

STALIN

We want to bomb them.

The Incurables (Part 2)

(SFX: AIR RAID SIRENS)

CRUMBLING / MILLIGAN
It's a Warsaw concerto warning, sir!

(CONCERTO BEGINS)

ANNOUNCER
Older listeners who have died for their country may remember that Rudolph Hess had come to England offering an armistice in the shape of a German sausage. Ignored by Churchill and actor's equity, Rudolph Hess, Hitlers Number Two—and I say that advisably—took off to Boots in Piccadilly.

SHOPKEEPER
Can I be of any assistance?

HESS / MILLIGAN
Ja! I want a thousand quarts of California syrup of figs.

SHOPKEEPER
Why did you leave it so long?

HESS / MILLIGAN
Somebody open a window.

SHOPKEEPER
Tell me, who is it for?

HESS / MILLIGAN
It's for Adolf Hitler.

SHOPKEEPER
I'm sorry sir, but we cannot serve the enemy in times of war.

HESS / MILLIGAN
You refuse to help ein sick man?

SHOPKEEPER
Oh, Hitler is sick?

HESS
You should see his carpet! Now, I demand to see your manager, Lord Halifax!

SHOPKEEPER
He doesn't work in Boots!

HESS / MILLIGAN
Okay, so he works in shoes! Thinks. <u>You</u> will sign the surrender sausage.

SHOPKEEPER
Oh no I won't!

HESS / MILLIGAN
Oh yes you will!

SHOPKEEPER
Oh no I won't! (audience joins in)

HESS / MILLIGAN
Oh yes you will!

SHOPKEEPER
Oh no I won't! (audience joins in)

HESS
Curse! Beaten by audience participation!

The Incurables (Part 2)

(SFX: DRAMATIC CHORD. SFX: HOWLS)

ANNOUNCER
Meanwhile, in the incurable ward, John was worried about a howling overdraft that had followed him up from St John's Wood.

JOHN
It's still out there, do you hear me? It's driving me mad. M-A-D mad, mad! K-A-T, cat. B-H-O-R-L-Z, balls. D-O-O-G-X, dog.

DOCTOR
He's having a bad spell. (audience groans) Oh, that poor overdraft. We obviously have to feed it money. A saucer of money could trap it.

JOHN
It. I-T, it.

(SFX: HOWLING, SAD VIOLIN)

ANNOUNCER
Disguising the saucer of money as a violin solo, they set off to trap the overdraft from the Midland, the listening bank with hearing aids switched off.

(SFX; HOWLING STOPS. YELLING AND BANGING. SHORT BREAK TO CATCH THEIR BREATH, THEN CONTINUES WITH YELLING AND BANGING.)

DOCTOR
Let's get it under the bed.

(SFX: CLONK! HOWLING CONTINUES)

DOCTOR
Fool, you've put it in the po.

MILLIGAN

Yes, it's safer in the P-O, sir.

DOCTOR

Not so loud. You don't want to attract burglars, do you?

PARTNER

Well, I don't mind a good looking one.

JOHN

Oh, shut up! Don't you all realise in two weeks we'll be dead? D-E-D, dead!

DOCTOR

D-E-A-D is dead.

JOHN

Oh, I'm sorry to hear that.

PARTNER

I say, according to my label it says that the Green Swan in its final stages can cause emotional traumas from the waist down darling.

(ALL SQUABBLE)

JOHN

Well, according to my label, it says get your hands off my knee darling. Or, you'll get the Duke of Edinburgh award for hello sailor.

ANNOUNCER

Dawn. (Sings dramatic chords) A military gentleman arrived at the park and addressed them through the microphone of his decontamination suit.

SGT. MAJOR / MILLIGAN

(drill voice) Stand at ease! I have been sent here by His Majesty the King. In appreciation of your work, I am empowered to raise you all to the peerage! Well done, the Gunners!

VOICE 1

Gunner? I say, that's a military term. So, we haven't been elevated to the peerage? We've been elevated to the army.

SGT. MAJOR / MILLIGAN

Yes. Correct. Your orders are to be parachuted behind enemy lines.

VOICE 2

What training do we get?

SGT. MAJOR / MILLIGAN

Stand on your beds!

VOICE 1

Alright.

SGT. MAJOR / MILLIGAN

Steady…. Jump!

VOICE 2

Oh.

(SFX: VARIOUS BOINGS)

SGT. MAJOR / MILLIGAN

It will be like that, only much higher. Congratulations.

VOICE 1

Thank you, sir.

SGT. MAJOR / MILLIGAN

Here are your wings.

(SFX: QUACKING)

VOICE 1

I say, they're still on the duck.

VOICE 2

Look here sergeant. I'm too young to die.

SGT. MAJOR / MILLIGAN

Alright, if you're too young to die, you might be old enough tomorrow. Ha ha ha, ha ha ha. Someone's gotta laugh at them.

VOICE 2

Look here. You're trying to take away my last fortnight of life with my incurable disease.

SGT. MAJOR / MILLIGAN

That's right.

VOICE 2

There's a lot one can do in a fortnight, you know. There's that NAAFI girl with the waterbed. I'm not going to throw it away on some boring useless war!

SGT. MAJOR / MILLIGAN

It is not a useless war! Listen to this!

(SFT: 'WE'LL MEET AGAIN' ON GRAMAPHONE.

VOICE 2

Okay, chummie, you listen to this.

(SFX: DONKEY LEADING INTO 'WE'LL MEET AGAIN')

ANNOUNCER
Meanwhile, a secret school for multiple Winston Churchill's was opened on Salisbury Plains.

MULTIPLE CHURCHILLS IN UNISON
All I can promise you is blood, sweat, and tears. And now, George Chisholme and his gentlemen of Jazz, some chicken, some stuffing.

(MUSICAL INTERLUDE)

McGONAGALL / MILLIGAN
Oh, The Incurables went up in a plane
And immediately were never seen again.
So where could these Incurables be?
Oh, dearie, dearie, dearie me.

ANNOUNCER
Oh, I say Mr McGonagall!

McGONAGALL / MILLIGAN
What do ye say there?

ANNOUNCER
Is anything worn under the kilt?

McGONAGALL / MILLIGAN
Aye. It's nearly dropping off. Wait til Saint Mary Whitehouse sees that.

ANNOUNCER
Is that why you wear an ankle-length sporran?

McGONAGALL / MILLIGAN
Och aye. Och nose. Och teeth. Oh, och-tober.

VOICE 3
Thank you.

McGONAGALL / MILLIGAN
Come inside the house and warm yourself by this cat. I'll just nail ye to the mantle-piece.

(SFX: HAMMERING)
Don't want you wearing out the chairs… Now I must start work on my new do-it-yourself poem.

(SFX: SAWING)
Oh, oh, oh oh oh. 'As I watched her wander o'er the heath, (SFX: SAWING) Black were the colour of my true love's teeth (SFX: SAWING) As I watched him wander through the fair (SFX: SAWING) Bald was the colour of the announcer's hair.

ANNOUNCER
That's a wonderful Scottish poem.

McGONAGALL / MILLIGAN
Oh, I love Scottish poetry. Do you like Burns?

ANNOUNCER
Yes!

McGONAGALL / MILLIGAN
Hold this poker.

ANNOUNCER
Ahh!

BBC VOICE
Mr McGonagall, I'm coming from the BBC.

The Incurables (Part 2)

McGONAGALL / MILLIGAN
Och!

BBC VOICE
We are willing to pay you to come to London to watch the Terry Wogan Show.

McGONAGALL / MILLIGAN
Great! Great! (calls) Ginny! Make me up an overnight sandwich!

GINNY
Aye, I'll put a clean nightshirt in it.

McGONAGALL / MILLIGAN
Now, while I'm away Ginny, do not let nae stranger cross the threshold.

GINNY
Dinna worry. He won't get out till he pays. Oh, what would I do without ma wee Willy?

McGONAGALL / MILLIGAN
Never mind that, what would I do without it?

GINNY
Say goodbye to the bairns.

McGONAGALL / MILLIGAN
Okay! Goodbye Angus. Goodbye Fiona. Goodbye Duncan. Goodbye Stewart. Goodbye Ian. Goodbye Jim. Goodbye Andrew. Goodbye Sandy. Goodbye Reuben…Reuben?

ANNOUNCER
That night McGonagall cancelled the Jewish milkman and bar-mitzvahed his horse.

SFX A SHOT !

McGONAGALL/MILLIGAN
Ohhh, it's the McGonagall culling season ! There'll only be one of me left soon ! Ahh dear! How shall I mate then? Ginny!

JENNY
Aye, aye ! Ma gud man ?

McGONAGALL
Open the door and let me in!

JENNY
We do not have a door, Jimmy!

MCGONAGALL
Ohh, I'll come through the window!

JENNY
We have no window !

McGONAGALL
I'll come down the chimney!

JENNY
What chimney?j

McGONAGALL
We must be grateful for four walls !

JENNY
Ye canna count, man! We only have two walls!

McGONAGALL
I'm glad to hear it!

JENNY
Why on earth is that?

McGONAGALL
It means I'm not deaf!

NARRATOR
There we must leave that charming domestic scene... In a BBC canteen, the manageress Gladys Stroke was speaking to the survivors of the last meal she had served, when she heard voices from inside a huge meat pie. Yum-yum!

STROKE
Is there anybody there?

PARACHUTIST
(muffled) Yes. We're survivors of a parachute drop over Germany.

(SFX: GROANING AND FARTING NOISES)

STROKE
What was that?

2ND PARACHUTIST
Oh don't worry, it was one of ours.

STROKE
Listen, I've had enough.

PARACHUTIST
You lucky woman.

MILLIGAN
Hello? Gladys? I'll have that big meat pie, yum yum.

STROKE
What sort of a day have you had?

MILLIGAN
I've had a Wednesday.

STROKE
Today is Friday.

MILLIGAN
It's been a funny sort of a Wednesday. Here. My trousers kept coming down.

STROKE
Trousers? Which side do you dress?

MILLIGAN
Near the window.

STROKE
That sounds like a Tuesday.

MILLIGAN
Listen. Starting to eat meat pie acting.

(SFX: PICKING UP CUTLERY)

2ND PARACHUTIST
Listen, stop that sound effect of picking up cutlery and listen. What was that?

MILLIGAN
It's just me listening.

PARACHUTIST
Look, don't eat us. We're contaminated.

MILLIGAN
Gladys! This pie is underdone. It's talking to me.

ANNOUNCER
Untroubled by the meat pie saga, members of the House of Lords discussed the war.

(ALL AD-LIB)

CHURCHILL
What about the war?

LORD 1 / MILLIGAN
It's not right. The Germans have started bombing Vera Lynn.

LORD 2
They're allowed to!

LORD 1 / MILLIGAN
No they're not. We wrote and told them 'no bombing allowed'. Well, not too loud.

LORD 3
But if they don't bomb loud enough, how will we know when they go off? Silent bombing could be dangerous.

LORD 1 / MILLIGAN
Not for the deaf!

LORD 2
I heard that.

LORD 1 / MILLIGAN
Why should blind people pay rates for street lighting?

LORD 3
Should we up the license fee?

LORD 1 / MILLIGAN
Up yours!

(SFX: ADLIB. DRAMATIC CHORD.)

CRUMBLING / MILLIGAN
Yes yes yes yes (continue). Mr. Prime Minister—I've decided I've been too much of a yes man.

CHURCHILL
Try no.

CRUMBLING / MILLIGAN
Yes. No, that's it, yes, no no.

CHURCHILL
Good. Pop down to the corner shop and get me some cigars.

CRUMBLING / MILLIGAN
No, sir. Right away.

CHURCHILL
Have The Incurables been dropped by parachute into Germany yet?

CRUMBLING / MILLIGAN
Yes sir. No, unfortunately the pilot overshot the dropping zone and dropped them in a meat pie. It's time for your broadcast to Germany, sir, to cover Hitler's recent downtown jazz forecast.

CHURCHILL
Will this shorten the war?

CRUMBLING / MILLIGAN
By about twelve inches, sir.

CHURCHILL
Ah. Twelve inches. I remember those days.

(SFX: AIR RAID SIRENS)

CHURCHILL
Take cover.

CRUMBLING / MILLIGAN
Sir, it's a ride of the Valkyries warning.

(SFX: VALKYRIES PLAYS)

CHURCHILL
Take cover, and Andrew's liver salts!

ANNOUNCER
So, Hitler's squadron of Wagner's Valkyries rained chorus after chorus upon the defenceless Albert Hall. By now, the man had eaten the giant meat pie, thus freeing the Incurables, who for the safety of the audience, are in a crate marked 'highly contagious' onboard a bomber off to drop them on Germany. They're discussing their plight.

PARACHUTIST 1
Well, chaps, what do you think of our plight?

PARACHUTIST 2
Well, we're lucky to have a plight in these hard times.

PARACHUTIST 1
What should we do with it then?

PARACHUTIST 2

First thing to do with a plight is paint it.

PARACHUTIST 3

Oh, for God's sake. Stop talking about painting our plight. It won't do any good. We're (sung) doom-doom-doom-doomed.

ANNOUNCER

Yes, doomed. Now we join the crew of the RAF bomber in a black comedy sequence.

RAF CREW

Pilot to Johnny. Pilot to Johnny. How's the rear gunner?

JOHNNY

Bert's dead.

RAF CREW

Are you certain?

JOHNNY

I'll just make sure. (SFX: GUNSHOT) Yes. Quite certain now.

RAF CREW

Never did like Bert. He's a messy eater. How's Philip, our navigator?

JOHNNY

He bought it. Guts everywhere.

RAF CREW

Oh, good, never did like Philip. Too stuck up.

JOHNNY

Well he certainly is stuck up now.

RAF CREW

How's Harry in the upper turret?

JOHNNY

Harry? Total wipeout, limbs everywhere.

RAF CREW

Good, good, never did like Harry. Wouldn't put his hand in his pocket.

JOHNNY

Well, yes, his hand's in his pocket now. God knows where his pocket is though.

RAF CREW

Good, good. Another quiet night, Johnny.

JOHNNY

Yes.

RAF CREW

Great fun.

JOHNNY

Isn't it.

RAF CREW

Prepare to drop The Incurables.

JOHNNY

I already dropped them, sir.

RAF CREW

Good, good. Never did like them. Stuck up lot.

JOHNNY
That's quite right. That's why I didn't attach a parachute to the crate.

RAF CREW
Good, good. Never saw them buy a round.

JOHNNY
No.

RAF CREW
Ok, let's head for home, Johnny.

(SFX: DRAMATIC MUSIC)

RAF CREW
Yes, good to have the old dramatic chords functioning again.

ANNOUNCER
As the Royal Household Incurables plunged to their death, the Incurables jumped out just before it hit the ground—

(SFX: CRASH NOISES)

ANNOUNCER
And were saved. Unfortunately, they were immediately eaten by a flock of green swans. Good night!

SFX: RADIO CRACKLING, TUNING ETC

GOEBBELS
Hello England ! Hello England ! This is downtown Berlin, home of jazz! Inviting you to get with it !
You are finished! Kaput! For you Tommy the war is over !

HITLER / MILLIGAN

Yah! They cannot even end ze doomed Milligan show without our musical number, Goebbels. The Milligan and his pals are kaput! It is curtains for them!

GOEBBELS

You have been sick on the curtains!

HITLER / MILLIGAN

Never mind ! Add it to my cleaning bill !

GOEBBELS

It is already enormous!

HIT.ER / MILLIGAN

I'm glad something is! Take it away man.. !

BOTH SING

Let's all go down the Strand...

OMNES

Seig Heil!

BOTH SING

Let's all go down the strand !

OMNES

Seig Heil !

GOEBBELS

Have a banana !

CHURCHILL

I haven't seen a banana in years !

ADOLPH / MILLIGAN
Then our U-Boat campaign is working!

CHURCHILL
No, it's not. It was down the Labour Exchange last week in Golders Green.

ADOLPH / MILLIGAN
That is Jewish propaganda!

CHURCHILL
And you could with a proper haircut!

ADOLPH / MILLIGAN
Oh yah? Well you listen to this... We will occupy ze Golders Green Empire! No more decedent shows like ze Milligatany Papers! It will be ze Hitler Papers!

CHURCHILL
Yes, the Hitler Wallpapers! Because that's about your level—paper hanging!

ANNOUNCER
And that's really all we have time for, listeners—Goodnight!

ADOLPH / MILLIGAN
I demand a recount! What gives with that Churchill? Can't you see he's drunk?! He is a drunken swine!! I am vegetarian! It works perfectly with the mercury mein Doctor is injecting! I will last a thousand years! If I do not shoot myself in 1945! Always a possibility... EVA!

EVA
Yah?

ADOLPH / MILLIGAN
You can get dressed now, mein leiber. We are going home...

(GRAMS IN STRONG)

THE END

Phew! It's over! A good show tonight! Lots of laughter! JOB DONE,..

Is it enough? Do we really want a second series? Can anyone stand it? Isn't that empty feeling preferable—all is possible but nothing is happening, you know what I mean?

Dreams don't have hard edges! But living nightmares do! Ouch! But at least you know you're alive!

Let's celebrate! Just for tonight, for God sake, whoever, whatever... Come on, John, if you feel high, be high. It is natural not product induced. You can always crash and burn later...

We have endured MONSTER MILLIGAN and SAINT MILLIGAN, and there have been kind moments... and kind of moments out of time when we were ONE! The cast, the audience, the world!! We touched the stars and numbered ourselves amongst them So thanks for that...

There is a life outside MILLIGAN. Let us venture forth and find it. For the sun will rise, another day will dawn and...

Ooooh! Och aye the Nooo!
Now ends this tale, a pretty stew
For end it must though we go on
Life's but the echo of a song....
My Bonny Lass my hearts with you!
My liver and kidneys I left at Crewe
At a wedding I left my own false teeth
Though regarding my kilt all's safe beneath!
Ohhhh! May all of you both kith and kin,
Now close this book, another chapter in your own lives to begin
Farewell! Farewell! Continue on!
It's time you wrote your own life's song!
Ooooohhhh ....
Fading quietly away, not to endure a lengthy stay....

www.ingramcontent.com/pod-product-compliance
Lightning Source LLC
Chambersburg PA
CBHW071004160426
43193CB00012B/1905